I Believed and Therefore I Spoke

Timothy T. Black, Jr.

PRESS

Table of Contents

Acknowledgments

I cannot express enough thanks to Almighty God for making all of this possible. Thank you, Lord, for humbling me. Many thanks go to my lovely wife, Denita, for going through all the pain and joy with me, and then for proofreading the manuscript over and over. I am forever grateful to Bootsie and Doug. And, finally, thanks to Don, Walton, and especially Clay for providing feedback on the early manuscript and for encouraging me.

CHAPTER 1

The Opening Question

M ost of us form our religious beliefs gradually as we travel life's journey. Those of us blessed enough to have been raised in Christian homes have a foundation for our beliefs laid down for us by our parents, church leaders, and fellow members of our churches. As we mature in the faith, God sometimes modifies our beliefs by what He reveals to us in His Word and through life's experiences.

In the year 2004 God allowed my family and me to experience things that completely altered my religious belief system. For many years I believed that Satan's power to prevent us from receiving the reward of heaven was limited to what he could accomplish through temptation. I believed that he had the ability to place temptations before us, but I don't think it was clear in my mind exactly how that worked.

During the last few years I began to understand that Satan has angels who do his work, just as God has angels who minister to us. But I had no idea the things that happened this past year were even remotely possible. I had no idea that an attack from Satan could be so personal. This is the story of a monumental struggle between my family and the forces of Satan and the victory we won through Jesus Christ.

However, this is more than just a story about an encounter with evil. This is also a story about a series of awesome encounters with God. Until very recently, I kept God inside a box. In my mind, there was a difference between the God of the Bible and the God who leads Christians today. I believed in a God who has the ability to do miraculous wonders for His children, and who actually once did that, but who does not perform miracles today. I believed in a Holy Spirit who worked miraculously through various gifts given to the early church, but who withdrew from active participation in the guidance of the church to watch from the throne of heaven. The God I believed in was a very well-behaved God whose modern-day activities were limited, as if He had been contained inside a box.

Well, I am here to proclaim to you that God cannot be contained within a box. The story I will relate to you is the account of how God exploded from the box into which I had placed Him and caused me to fall to my knees in the presence of His glory and awesome power.

In 2 Corinthians 4:13, the apostle Paul addresses his motivation for preaching the gospel of Christ: "And since we have the same spirit of faith, according to what is written, 'I believed and therefore I spoke,' we also believe and therefore speak." In quoting Psalm 116:10 in this passage, Paul is telling us that he essentially could not help but proclaim the gospel of Christ because his faith had been so bolstered by his experiences in the Lord. Until very recently, I could not claim to understand Paul's message in this passage. Today, however, I think I fully understand. My recent personal encounters with the forces of Satan and with our magnificent God have affected me so deeply and profoundly I cannot keep from telling my story.

For me, it all started one chilly day in late February 2004, but as I was soon to learn, it had actually begun much earlier for my eighteen-year-old son, Anderson. In the evenings, my wife Denita and I usually walked up and down the road on which we live. Usually one or both of our children would accompany us. On this particular February evening Denita was not feeling well, so Anderson and his fourteen-year-old sister, Victoria, walked with me. I realized later that Anderson had been waiting for such an opportunity to approach me about something that had been on his mind for a long time. I would learn later that he had wanted to talk to me without his mom being present, for reasons you will see later.

After we had been walking no more than two or three minutes that evening, Anderson said to me, "I've got a question for you."

"Okay," I said, expecting some easily answered question about something he had learned in school, or cars, or girls, or anything else a teenage boy might be concerned about. The question he asked was definitely not what I was expecting.

"Do you believe dead people roam the earth?"

I was surprised but still managed to answer smugly, "Well, I don't think so. I couldn't rule out that possibility, but through study I've convinced myself that when people die, there is a place where their souls go. They're not free to just roam around."

"Oh."

There was silence as we continued to walk. I thought to myself, *I don't think he asked this question to find out what I believe on this subject, because he already knows what I believe.* I was fairly certain of that because we had discussed this very topic several times both at home and at church. But, then, don't most of us forget most of what we have ever learned? I realized he wasn't going any further with the conversation on his own, so I asked, very innocently, "Why? Do you think you've seen somebody?"

I actually thought I was going to hear him tell me about some experience he had had that made him think that maybe there was such a thing as ghosts. Once again, his response was very unexpected: "I can see things other people can't see."

"What do you mean?" Suddenly, for me, this went from a conversation to pass the time as we walked to something much more serious.

"There are certain places I go where I see people. I think they're dead people. Well, I don't always see them. Sometimes I just sense that they are there. And I can sense when other people are close to me. Like, if somebody is behind me, I can tell they are there without hearing them. I just feel them there."

At this point, Victoria exclaimed, "He's right! I can never sneak up on him! I've tried and tried, but I have never been able to sneak up on him."

Anderson once told his mom that he was able to hear everything in the house from his upstairs bedroom, even quiet whispering downstairs, so I figured he probably had a very keen sense of hearing, and that explained why his sister could never sneak up on him. So I said something to him about how he must have very keen hearing, and he might be hearing things going on around him that were so subtle they weren't registering with his conscious mind as sounds. Near the end of our walk, I brought up this particular subject again by explaining to him how "just feeling things" is a very foreign notion to me. At this point, he moved closer to me as we continued to walk and said, "Do you mean that you don't feel me being closer to you right now?"

I answered, "No. I only know you are closer because I can see and hear you. Do you feel that we are closer together now than we were?"

His tone of voice as he replied "Yes!" made it sound as though he were talking to somebody from another planet. And I guess he was right in a way. Teenagers and parents are often miles apart in their thinking, but on this particular subject I was feeling like we were worlds apart.

But I have deviated from the main part of the story and the most important part of this conversation. I had very quickly and easily explained away in my mind Anderson's notion that he just "senses" when people are there by attributing this ability to an especially keen sense of hearing. But that didn't explain what Anderson was telling me about seeing dead people. So I asked him, "Where are some places where you've seen these people?"

"Well, Grandpa and Grandmama's house is one place where I've seen them." My parents live in a house that was built in 1906, and it is one of those houses that might persuade somebody that ghosts really do exist. There are lots of sounds in the house, doors sometimes close on their own, and other objects sometimes seemingly move on their own. So my first thought, when Anderson started explaining about the "people" he saw in the house, was that when he was very young his imagination had conjured up these "ghosts."

Anderson went on to explain that in one upstairs bedroom he could see two women. These women were always in the same part of the room. When I asked him how they interacted with him, he said when he would enter the room they would just look at him. He said that if he moved toward them, they sometimes would move toward him and sometimes they would move away from him. I asked him if they talked to him, and he said no. I also asked him if they were always there, even if somebody else was there with him. He said he could see the women in the room every time he was there. He had taken other people into the room with him, such as his cousins, but he never let on to anybody what he was doing. He wanted to see if it made any difference whether another person was present. He said it didn't matter; he always saw the women.

Anderson then said that there were other spirits in his grandparents' house and that some of them he could only sense rather than see. He then told me about two other places where he had seen "people," as he called them. One was Ft. Morgan, an old coastal fort near Mobile. The other place was on a part of our mountain land. It takes a fairly strenuous climb to reach the area to which Anderson referred, but he had been there several times, as I had also, and he said there were always fifteen or twenty of these "people" just standing around up there.

One interesting point Anderson made as he described all of these "people" he had seen was that he had wondered if maybe he was schizophrenic. He said he had even researched schizophrenia on the Internet in order to assure himself that he didn't have a mental problem. He said he had learned that schizophrenic people hear voices, so he had concluded that he wasn't schizophrenic. I have to say that I once knew somebody who was paranoid/schizophrenic, and Anderson was acting nothing like this person. Whenever I had conversations with the schizophrenic young man I once knew, it was very clear to me that I was talking to somebody with severe mental problems, even if he was taking his medication at the time. He constantly talked about very bizarre things and strange visions he had seen. But Anderson never exhibited the kind of behavior I had always associated with mental illness. As he described these spirits to me, he seemed very rational and normal. I felt like he was just matter-of-factly describing some things he had seen. So, even though when our conversation began I was somewhat skeptical, by the end of the conversation I knew I believed what my son was telling me.

I need to interject at this point that I come from a Church of Christ background that generally does not accept the idea of spirits roaming the earth. I have always accepted ghost stories as myths, legends, or the result of overactive imaginations. Also, I am an engineer by profession, a group that is known (maybe even sometimes despised) for our tendency to overanalyze problems and to rely heavily on concrete facts and logic to arrive at conclusions and solve problems. I don't say this to promote my own intellect or to boast about myself. I say this to make the point that if this had been somebody other than my own son telling me these things, I probably would have explained them away. But this was my son, and I could see no reason for him to make up such a wild story.

Victoria, of course, was as surprised by what she had heard during our walk as I was. After returning home, she told her mom all about it. A short while later, Denita asked me about the conversation Anderson and I had, and I then asked Anderson in private if he intended to share his experiences with his mom. He explained to me that he had not wanted to discuss all of this with her because he was afraid she would become upset. His mom had been having some serious health problems, and he was afraid she couldn't handle this kind of news. This is why he had waited for the opportunity to speak to me without his mom present. I assured him that she could handle this, so he repeated for her all the things he had told me.

CHAPTER 2

We Have Our Own Questions

Over the next few days, Denita and I questioned Anderson further about the things he could "see," as we tried to gain a better understanding of what was happening. We ignorantly attributed Anderson's "ability," as I came to call it, to God. We felt this was some gift from God that Anderson needed to learn how to use properly. We were to learn later how foolish we were in thinking this.

About two weeks after the initial conversation I had with Anderson, he announced to us that he had a girlfriend. This was an uncomfortable announcement for him to make, because we had been teaching our children that we thought the courtship approach to relationships was a better approach than traditional dating. We felt the risk of becoming involved in a sinful physical relationship or a hurtful emotional relationship was much lower in courtship. We had made attempts to instill in our children the importance of avoiding a serious relationship until they were ready for marriage. Because our children were homeschooled, it was easy to implement such an approach, but we realized that once our children began work or college there was a real possibility that they would meet somebody and begin a relationship that would negate all of the values we had instilled in them.

Anderson had been working at a fast food restaurant for about two years when he met a girl there with whom he became emotionally involved. We reminded him of our beliefs on dating and how he should be careful in this relationship to do things God's way and not to sin. He was quick to let us know that those were our beliefs and not his. This was the beginning of some significant tension between us, but we had no idea at the time that we were dealing with a relationship that went beyond the normal physical and emotional attraction between a young man and a young woman.

From this point on, we saw a noticeable change in Anderson's attitudes and behavior. Actually, we had noticed a change in his attitudes over the previous two years. He had gradually become more rebellious and less tolerant of behavior, attitudes, and tastes that were different from his own. He had begun having angry outbursts, listening to music that was more and more rebellious, and pushing the limits on the kind of clothing we would permit him to wear. Anderson had never had any real friends. Every attempt on our part to place him in situations where he could develop friendships resulted in his rejection of all potential friends. He simply could not tolerate anybody who did not think, act, and dress exactly as he did. We spent many hours attempting to counsel him on his attitudes and behavior, but to no avail. Denita had mentioned to me several times over the last few years that she sensed something was not right with Anderson. I just attributed it to his immaturity and to the fact that he was a teenager. But we would soon learn we were battling more than simple teenage rebellion.

Over the course of the next few days, we learned a little more about Anderson's "ability." He told us how he was able to leave his body, go somewhere else, and then return to his body. This is called astral projection or astral traveling. He told us about how he had confirmed this ability when he left his body during his sleep one night and went to be with "somebody." He wouldn't tell us whom. This person told him the next day that they had actually talked to him, even though he was at home in bed. This person told him what time this had occurred, and he knew it was the correct time because he awoke upon returning to his body and looked at the time on the clock. It corresponded with the time given him the next day by the person he had visited.

Over the next two weeks or so, Anderson began spending more and more time with his girlfriend, Mary (not her real name). We told him it was not right for him to be spending so much time with a girl. He continuously reminded us that our beliefs on dating were not his beliefs. He became more and more resentful of our attempts to have him abide by our rules on where he could go and when he should be home. He talked a lot about how he couldn't wait until he was able to move out of the house so that he didn't always have somebody nosing in his business and telling him what to do.

One Saturday he went to the mall with Mary and we told him to be home by a certain time in the afternoon. He came home about thirty minutes later than that, and when I asked him why, his reply was "'cause." I told him that was not a good enough answer, and a very heated discussion between parents and son ensued in our kitchen. Denita made some comment about telling Mary's dad about our displeasure with the two of them spending so much time together and about Anderson arriving home later than he was told. Anderson's response was, "If you do that, you'll find out something you don't want to know."

"Like what?" Denita asked.

"You just don't want to do that."

"Why don't you tell us what it is we'll find out if we call him?"

Anderson became extremely angry and wanted to leave the house, but I stood between him and the door. Denita and I didn't want him driving his car while he was angry. He actually balled up his fist as if he was going to hit me, but he didn't. Denita put her loving, motherly arms around him and finally got him to calm down. She convinced him to talk to us about what he had said. He agreed to do that, so we went into the living room and sat down and had a conversation that redefined the world for us.

CHAPTER 3

The Day My World Was Redefined

I need to preface what I am about to tell you with a brief explanation of my religious background. Because of my beliefs, I was not very in tune to many aspects of the spiritual warfare that is being engaged all around us. Several years ago I read and studied a book by Joe Beam titled *Seeing the Unseen: A Handbook on Spiritual Warfare,*[1] and had arrived at a better understanding of the nature of Satan and how he wars against Christians. Prior to reading that book, I was convinced that Satan worked against us through simple temptation—that is, he knows my weaknesses and he makes sure something is put in place to exploit those weaknesses. I never really considered the mechanics of how that actually might be done, but after reading the book by Joe Beam, I could see that Satan does much of his work through his angels and demons. These might actually be one in the same, but I'll leave that for others to debate.

My religious background just would not allow me to give serious consideration to the possibility that people in modern times can actually come into contact with beings in the spirit world through occultic practices or other means. I also could not convince myself that demon possession in modern times is possible, although I could not entirely rule out that possibility because of people like Adolf Hitler and

Charles Manson. As a consequence of my ignorance, I was ill-equipped to handle the situation which is the subject of this story.

The conversation with Anderson began with him telling us that not only could he see spirits, but there was one spirit in particular he both saw and communicated with. He told us this spirit's name was Han. During this conversation and others we had with Anderson over the next few days, we learned that Han was a spirit Anderson had known since he was a very young child. "For as long as I can remember," was the way he worded it. According to Anderson, Han was a dead person. In life, he had been a Nazi, but one of an elite group of Nazis.

Anderson told us that, according to Han, the Nazis had learned how to summon demons to possess people. Han also told him that Hitler was Satan, and that Hitler's castle was a place where demons were summoned into the world. Han had been one of the demon-possessed Nazis and one of those who summoned demons. He told Anderson he had gotten rid of his demon and now his duty was to protect members of Denita's family who were originally from Germany. Initially, when Anderson told us this story, he said Han was one of his mom's grandfathers. During a later conversation, we told Anderson it was not possible for Han to have been one of his grandfathers. Denita's family emigrated to America in the late 1800s. Anderson replied, "Well, he was some kind of relative." Denita later recalled how anytime there was a conversation about tracing family history, Anderson would tell his mom, "Yeah, and you're probably related to a Nazi!"

We also learned in later conversations that Anderson had found websites on the Internet that confirmed in his mind the information from Han about the Nazis summoning demons. He said he even learned from these websites that near the end of the war, the U.S. Government sent exorcists into Germany to exorcise the demons from the Nazis. We were curious about exactly how Anderson communicated with this Han, and how often he saw Han. In later conversations, we learned that Han was not always with Anderson, but that Han would appear from time to time and talk to Anderson. Anderson also told us that he could cause Han to appear just by asking for him. At this time, Denita and I were so ignorant of demons that we did not even consider the possibility that Han was a familiar spirit. In fact, we didn't even know what a familiar spirit was. But more on that later.

Anderson went on to explain to us how, when he was a little child, he saw demons but did not fear them because Han was there to explain these kinds of things to him. He emphasized to us that this was Han's function. Anderson wasn't afraid of any demon he saw because Han told him that the demon wasn't after him. At some point in this conversation, his mom asked him what all of this had to do with us calling Mary's dad, which was what got the conversation started in the first place. He said he was getting to that. He said he had to tell us these other things first so that we would understand what he was going to tell us about Mary.

So Anderson continued, and he informed us that he now had demons who were "around him" and that they "bothered" him. He denied that they actually possessed him in any way. He said he had the ability to keep them at bay with Han's help, but he did admit that these demons had influence over his behavior. In fact, he attributed his angry outburst that led to this conversation to one of the demons. In later discussions with him, we learned that he always had at least one demon "around" him, but there were usually three and sometimes more. He told us he had to constantly fight against them because they wanted to possess him. And he described the three most prominent demons to us. Actually, he was not sure that these were actually demons. He said he referred to them that way because he didn't know what they were. He just knew they were evil. He said one demon was a demon of anger and could cause him to be very angry if he allowed it; another was a sadistic spirit that would like to kill just for the sake of killing. He was vague in his description of the third one, but he said it was another demon of anger, and it was different somehow from the first one. Anderson said that after he was baptized and saved, he prayed for four months for God to take all this from him but He didn't, so he began to turn against God. I'm sure it's not surprising to you that we were very concerned at this point, but what might surprise you is that we were not concerned that our son was mentally ill. We were concerned that he was actually being influenced by demons.

After explaining to us that he had these demons, Anderson went on to describe to us something that had happened to him a couple of times while driving his car. Of all the things he told us that day, this was the hardest for me to believe, but I must emphasize to you that I did come to believe that this actually happened. Anderson told us that one recent day, he was driving down Interstate 565 in Huntsville when something took control of his car. He had no control over the steering, accelerator, or brakes. He said his CD player stuck on a single note. It didn't stop playing, and it didn't skip or play the same note over and over. It played a single note throughout this entire episode. Anderson said as he lost control over the car it accelerated instantly to over 100 miles per hour, and he was headed for the rear end of an 18-wheeler.

Interestingly, and this really stood out in his mind, the car didn't vibrate at those high speeds and the engine didn't sound like it was running any faster. He expected to hear more noise from the wind or from the friction between tires and pavement, but there was no change in the way the car sounded. Just before hitting the 18-wheeler, Anderson took his hands off the steering wheel and "concentrated on the thing" that had control of his car. At the last second, he grabbed the steering wheel and was able to regain control of the car and swerve around the 18-wheeler. He said the same thing happened, without the involvement of an 18-wheeler, about two weeks later. The car instantly accelerated to over 100 miles per hour, the CD player stuck on a single note, and he had no control over the car. Once again, he removed his hands from the steering wheel, "concentrated" on what was controlling the car, and regained control. I understood him to be saying that he somehow mentally fought back the demon that was trying to kill him.

Of course, none of what Anderson described to us made any sense, and we questioned him fairly extensively. How could the car instantly go from 70 to 100 miles per hour? How could it not vibrate? How could it not make any more noise when it went faster? Was he sure this was actually happening, or was one of the demons causing him to think it was happening as a way of scaring him? His response was that it was actually happening, and why couldn't it? Angels have control over natural phenomena, so why couldn't demons?

I had a very hard time understanding how and why such things could happen. For a while I believed Anderson had been deceived into thinking his car was speeding and he had no control over it. But a few weeks later, after hearing Anderson's car story, one of the ladies in our congregation told me something she had never told anyone except her husband, and she had only told him very recently. It seems that about twenty-five years ago, she was driving her car and with her was her infant son. She said she rounded a curve in the road at a normal rate of speed and suddenly lost control of the car. Her hands were on the steering wheel, but she could not steer. She also lost control of the accelerator and the brakes. They did not respond when pressed with her feet. She could see that the car was going to leave the road and crash into a tree. She didn't know what else to do, so she just let go of the steering wheel, closed her eyes, and prayed for God's help. Well, God did help. The car straightened up and slowed to a stop in the road. She was then able to drive the car, and nothing like this ever happened again. To this day, she believes something was trying to kill her and God saved her.

By now, we had been talking with Anderson for well over an hour, and he finally came to the point he wanted to make about Mary. He was right about us needing all the other information in order to understand what he was about to tell us. For nearly two years Anderson had been working a part-time job at a fast food restaurant, and Mary had been working there for about a year. Anderson told us that when Mary started working there, he knew the first time he saw her that she could also see spirits. It turns out that people who have the ability to see things in the spirit world instantly know when they have met somebody else with that ability. They don't have to talk about it, they just know.

Later, Anderson would tell us the same thing happened when he met one of his teachers at school. He also became acquainted with seven other students at school who had this ability. In every case, he knew instantly that the other person could see spirits, and each of the others instantly understood the same thing about Anderson. No conversation on the topic ever had to take place.

After telling us about Mary, Anderson asked us, "Do you remember me telling you about how I went to somebody during the night while I was in bed?"

"Yes," we both answered.

"That was Mary," he said. "I went to her house that night because I knew a spirit was bothering her. I went to her room and forced the spirit to leave."

Anderson therefore thought he had the ability to fight against demons. By the end of this conversation, I was convinced that Anderson was not imagining anything he had told us, and I also was convinced that he was not mentally ill.

CHAPTER 4

Spirits in My Parents' House?

The discussion in our living room that day was just the beginning of the conversations Denita and I had with Anderson. In later conversations we learned more about the demons Anderson saw, and he explained more fully to us the strange interaction among Mary, her demons, and himself. Anderson insisted that he didn't have any special ability and that anybody can see spirits with some practice. Anderson also gave us more details concerning the teacher he had mentioned to us.

Anderson had told us before that one of his teachers during his first year of college was a shaman. We were somewhat concerned that he seemed to have struck up a friendship with this teacher and that he seemed to be so interested in her religious beliefs, but we were too ignorant and naive at this time about spiritual warfare and Satan's tactics to be alarmed to the appropriate extent. We eventually learned that he had established a friendship with this teacher because she also had the ability to see spirits. Anderson reminded us that when you have that ability you know when you've met somebody else with the ability without the exchange of any verbal communication. So Anderson and this teacher knew the first time they saw one another that they both had these extrasensory abilities.

During one of our conversations with Anderson, he told us he had learned that people with the ability to see spirits often have the ability to practice astral projection, and he found an Internet website that described how to accomplish the feat. He told us later his shaman teacher at school taught him more perfectly how to project himself. She even demonstrated it for him at school.

When we asked Anderson to tell us about other places where he had seen spirits, he told us there are many spirits at Civil War battle-fields. He knows that because we have visited many of them over the years. He explained to us how there were various places where he could see portals or doorways that spirits use to travel between hell and earth. My impression is that he did not know for sure the demons were coming from hell, but that he did know they were coming from somewhere in the spirit world. He said one of those portals is at Ft. Morgan, an old coastal fort that was used to defend the entrance to Mobile Bay. When he visited Ft. Morgan several years earlier, he walked into one of the dark passageways in the fort and saw the gateway, with spirits coming and going through it. He said he left the passageway and then went back in, just to make sure he wasn't imagining things. He still saw the spirits.

Once, while discussing the spirits in my parents' house, Anderson said his grandmother had unleashed several spirits during a remodeling project when she opened a fireplace in her house that had been covered up for many years. He explained that a long time ago, somebody had sealed up spirits in that fireplace intentionally. Later, when we questioned him on how it was possible for physical things to restrain spirits, he told us that some spirits can take on any shape, attach themselves to physical objects, and serve as barriers to other spirits. He said that such a thing had happened in our woods. He asked me, "Do you remember me telling you about the spirits wandering around in our woods?" When I replied that I did remember (how could I ever forget?) he said those spirits had been restrained within a barrier formed by a spirit that had attached itself to trees. When one of the trees fell one day, the barrier was broken and the spirits were released, but he didn't understand why they would just mill around in that one area. When I asked him what those spirits did when he approached them, he said they just stared at him.

In other discussions about the spirits in my parents' house, Anderson told us that only one of the spirits in their house talked to him. The others could only be seen and made no attempt to communicate. This spirit told Anderson it had tried to talk to my dad, but he was "too closed up," Anderson's term for people who are not open to the idea of spirits or who are not able to see them. He said the spirit had tried to talk to my mom, but she became scared and the spirit left her alone. Later, when I asked her if she remembered such a thing happening, she said she didn't.

Throughout all of the conversations we had with Anderson, we realized it was very important to him that we believe the things he was telling us. He was emphatic that all of these things had really happened. If we had approached all of this as if he had a mental illness, he would have broken off all communication with us on the subject, and he most certainly would not have stood for psychiatric or other medical treatment. But this wasn't really a problem, as Denita and I believed every word of what our son told us.

When we discussed these things with Anderson, it was never like having a conversation with a mentally ill person. He always conversed with us in a very normal way. In one of the many books I would later read on demon possession and the occult, a minister who had seen many schizophrenic people and many who were possessed by demons explained that it is usually very easy to tell the difference between the two.[1] The true schizophrenic cannot help but talk about the things he sees and hears, which are often extremely wild and unbelievable, while the demon-possessed person will likely not talk at all about the things he sees. The reason for this is that demons benefit from remaining hidden. As long as they don't reveal themselves, they can continue to use and torment their victims without hindrance.

CHAPTER 5

My Son Leaves Home

One morning, just a few days after our fateful conversation in the living room, Anderson overslept and his mom had to wake him so he wouldn't be late for school. He quickly dressed and sailed out of the house, but on the way out he paused long enough to tell his mom that he had been up all night and would explain why later. He said it was something she needed to know. Later, Anderson called his mom to explain. He said he didn't want to talk about this in front of Victoria because he didn't want to scare her. He told his mom that he had been up all night battling a demon that was trying to harm all of us. He said when he came home later he would give his mom and me all of the details.

When Anderson got home he told us he had been sitting at his computer in his bedroom late that night when he sensed an evil spirit behind him. When he turned around, he saw the spirit. He said the spirit told him it was going to Victoria's bedroom to kill her. He said he then sat down on the floor and concentrated on the evil thing that was in the room with him, and his spirit left his body. He said he was able to see his body still sitting on the floor, but he was also able to confront this evil spirit and stand between it and Victoria's room. He told us he had help in this battle. He said Han was there, but that he didn't really do anything. Anderson said he got help from some "good" spirits, and as long as they were standing beside him, he could keep the evil spirit from entering Victoria's room. When the spirit realized it couldn't enter her room, it tried to go downstairs to kill Denita and me, and Anderson and his helper spirits blocked the way again.

Anderson said that finally, after several hours, the helper spirits forced the evil spirit back into his room and essentially held it captive there. He eventually got to sleep for an hour or two, and he said that when he left to go to school that morning the evil spirit was still in his room but was being guarded by the "good spirits." He told us that when he came home that afternoon, he could tell before he got out of his car that the evil spirit was no longer in his room.

It's interesting that later I would read in the book *Witch Doctor*, by Dr. Lester Sumrall, this statement by Arlindo Barbosa de Oliveira, a man who had been a Macumba witch doctor in Brazil for forty years and was possessed by as many as three hundred demons, but later became a believer in Jesus Christ: "...devils do respect authority. All spirits have a certain category. When a spirit meets another of lesser degree, he commands him, and when he meets one of higher degree, he bows to him. *The spirit who belongs to you always tries to protect you from other spirits who would like to take you away from him.*"[1]

This quote by the witch doctor is just one of many accounts of occultic oppression or demon possession I have read containing details remarkably similar to the details of Anderson's story. This is yet another thing that convinces me that Anderson was not making up any of this. There are many, many documented cases very similar to Anderson's, and in all of the cases I have read, the oppressed person was delivered by God. But at this point in the story, I didn't know anything about demons, much less anything about deliverance from demons.

You might be wondering how Denita and I reacted to hearing this story about a demon in our house attempting to kill us. Weren't we afraid? Weren't we afraid for Victoria? Why didn't we gather up our belongings, leave the house, and take Victoria with us? If we believed all of this was real, why didn't we take action? Well, the truth is I was a little afraid as I heard this story, and I was truly alarmed to think that there were evil spirits with evil intentions in my house. But at the same time part of me rationalized that this demon wasn't really out to kill any of us. This was just another way these spirits bothered Anderson.

Denita and I discussed that possibility together, and we both eased our minds with the same rationalization. Yet there was still that little bit of nagging doubt. What if this demon really was out to kill us? I also had the thought go through my mind more than once that perhaps this demon would work through Anderson to kill us. I even briefly entertained the thought that Anderson was mentally ill, and that he might just go berserk one day and kill us all. In the end, however, my rationalizations won out over my fears.

But what about Victoria? Wasn't she afraid? She wasn't afraid because we didn't tell her about this. Since we had convinced ourselves that there was no real reason to fear, we saw no need to tell Victoria. Why make her afraid when it was unnecessary? It's at times like this when you hope and pray that you are doing the right thing. It's also at times like this that you realize you are faced with situations for which you are very ill-equipped. You realize that life's training ground doesn't always give you the skills you need, and sometimes you just have to turn everything over to God. That is exactly what Denita and I did in this situation; we prayed for God's protection over us and our children, and we tried to have courage.

It was during this period of time when I was reeling from my family's recent experiences that I bought a book on demonology. I had decided I didn't know nearly enough about demons and demon possession. I needed to read about experiences similar to the one my family was now having. I didn't want to read one of the many books explaining how it is not possible for people to be demon possessed in modern times, because I already knew all of those arguments. While shopping at a Christian bookstore one day, I discovered a book by a German, Kurt E. Koch, titled *Demonology Past and Present, Identifying and Overcoming Demonic Strongholds*.[2] I was intrigued by the author's assertion that demon possession most often occurs because the possessed person has been immersed in a sinful activity that allows Satan or his demons to gain access into the person's being. Particularly fascinating to me was the link Koch had seen between the occult and demon possession in his worldwide travels and ministry.

This was the first time I had read convincing evidence that occultism is not just a game. Koch presents the case that through the use of seances, ouija boards, and other devices and practices, it is possible for people to come into contact with the spirit world and to open the door to demon possession. The book by Koch also discusses a concept I would later learn is known as generational curses, though at this time the significance of such a thing in Anderson's life escaped me.

I now understand Koch was explaining that many times people are influenced by demons because an ancestor practiced occultism and opened the door to demons that would torment the same family for generations. Denita and I recalled people in past generations on both sides of the family who had the ability to know future events were going to happen, or could sense certain things occurring with a family member hundreds of miles away. We began to see that these kinds of abilities can all be placed under the general heading of occultism.

Not too long after reading this book I was rear-ended at a traffic light. It was April 13, 2004. The car I was driving was totaled. It seemed as though Satan was intensifying his attack on my family and me. He knew the stress I was already under because of Anderson, and now it seemed that he wanted to turn it up a notch. As it turned out, the car wreck was one of those blessings in disguise. As a precaution, I visited my doctor after the wreck and he ordered X-rays to check for spinal damage. There was no injury from the wreck, but the attending radiologist discovered I had a form of arthritis in my spine. A few weeks later, I had a physical examination during which my doctor discovered that I had lost the Achilles reflex in my right leg. He recommended I see a neurosurgeon. The loss of the reflex was probably related to the arthritis. He said I needed an evaluation of what kind of nerve damage I might have as a result of the arthritis. By the time I saw the neurosurgeon, I had developed pain in my right leg. No damage from the accident was visible from the MRI, but the doctor prescribed physical therapy anyway because he noticed a slightly deteriorated disk in my lower spine. The therapy relieved the pain in my leg, and the regimen of exercises strengthened my back and helped the pain I have suffered with for thirty years.

As positively as everything turned out with the car wreck, it still created extra stress for me, and then I came home from work on April 16 to find that Anderson had become very angry during the day and wanted to leave home for a while. Throughout this period of time when we were learning all these things about Anderson, his anger and rebellion and callousness toward us increased day by day. Every day he reminded us that all he wanted to do was get out of the house.

Anderson previously explained to us that the reason he treated us with such callousness was because this was the way he had to behave toward the demons that followed him around. He said the worst thing you can do if you see a demon is be afraid of it. So over time he had developed this callous attitude toward his demons that spilled over into his attitude toward people. And it wasn't just his attitude toward his parents that had soured. He expressed a vicious disdain toward other members of the family, including aunts, uncles, cousins, and our church family. When I say church family, I really mean family. The church I preached for at that time was very small in number, only four families meeting together in an old rented store in the country. I was the preacher—what most would call a lay preacher—mostly by default because nobody else would do it. That is not to say I did it grudgingly. I actually enjoyed it, though it could be quite a burden to bear at times. Well, Anderson now believed that everybody in our church was looking down on him and judging him, but for what he never really explained. He began telling his mom and me that the others were hypocrites.

By now we had become extremely concerned about Anderson. We had a long discussion with him the evening he left. We reminded him that we loved him and there was nothing he could do that would make us stop loving him. He drove away without even telling us where he was going. He just said he had somewhere he could go. He had a cell phone, so we knew we could call him if we needed to, so we let him go without pressing him for details. Denita and I cried and prayed a lot that night. The next day we bought a car to replace the one that had been wrecked. The Lord blessed us that day and made the car purchase very easy. It was a welcome relief.

CHAPTER 6

We Begin to Find Answers

Anderson came back home the next Monday evening, April 19, and we sat on our front porch and had a long discussion. For the first time, I felt like I wasn't really talking to my son. He seemed like a completely different person. It's hard to describe the look of insolence he had on his face. I had prepared what I wanted to say to him. The main thing I wanted him to know was that the time had come for him to either move out or stay and conduct himself in such a manner that our family could have some peace. There had been no real peace in our house for several weeks. I had even prepared a list of rules that he was going to have to agree to live by if he decided to stay with us. But first I felt like we needed to pray together, so we did.

After we prayed I began with the questions. The first question was why he was not at church on Sunday morning, to which he replied that he just didn't want to be there. When I asked him if he attended church somewhere else he said no. Next, Denita and I wanted to know where he had been staying. He told us that on Friday night he had parked his car behind our church building and slept in the car. The other nights he spent at a friend's house. He expressed to us his lack of faith in God, and he again expressed his dislike of Christians. We asked him if he knew where he was going to go if he did not straighten out his life and give it to God. His response was very chilling: "To hell, I guess."

It is my belief that during this conversation, it was not Anderson who was talking to us. Instead, the demons he thought he could control were actually speaking to us through his mouth. Out of the blue, Anderson attacked our friendship with Bootsie Moore, a lady who has as close a relationship with her Lord as anybody could have. He said she wasn't really a Christian. The demons controlling him at this time knew the future and what was going to happen. That is the reason they attacked Bootsie's character through Anderson. These future events to which I refer will unfold later in this story.

It was as if Anderson wanted to attack anything that was good. He also told us people always ran over him whenever he tried to do good. Being good always backfired on him. One example he gave us was when he beat up the boyfriend of a girl he had tried to help. This happened in the parking lot where Anderson and the girl both worked. She had been raped by her boyfriend and Anderson tried to help her get legal assistance. The boyfriend confronted Anderson and Anderson said he had to beat him up. It was as if we were having a conversation with someone devoid of any moral and religious training. If Anderson had come to us about the girl's problem, we would have counseled him on how better to handle the situation and how to find legal help for the girl. But coming to us about anything probably was not at the top of his list of things he wanted to do.

Anderson told us he had done other things that were much worse than beating up somebody. He wouldn't elaborate, but he told us he had done things at school for which he thought he could never be forgiven. We couldn't imagine what he might have done at school that was that bad, but nevertheless we tried to convince him that God is gracious and merciful and there is no sin so bad He will not forgive it. Anderson didn't buy any of it. I am convinced now that Satan persuaded him to believe there are sins that cannot be forgiven.

Finally, after going around in circles with Anderson for a very long time, we gave him the choice of staying with us and respecting our authority or leaving. He chose to leave. We allowed him to take whatever he wanted out of his room, including clothing, blankets, and a pillow, and then watched him drive away. It was the saddest event of my life. Denita and I cried and prayed practically all night.

Denita said all she could think of was her little boy sleeping in a car, because we were sure he did not have a place to stay. We were locked in a monumental conflict with Satan, and it looked like he was winning the battle.

We never felt like we were fighting this battle against evil without God's help, but we also had not seen a lot of evidence up to that point that He was intervening on our behalf. That would all soon change in such a dramatic way that my entire system of belief would be turned upside down.

During the next few days we felt like Anderson had died. No, it was worse than that. It was as if he were spiritually dead, but his physical body was still there, as if to torment us. I went to work and tried to carry on as if nothing was wrong, but it was very hard to concentrate on my job. My burden seemed extra heavy because I felt like I couldn't discuss my problems. I confided in one person because I felt like somebody needed to know what was going on, in case I started missing a lot of work. I chose the person most likely to be open-minded and non-judgmental. Denita asked me how I could function at all at work. I told her it was hard, but at least work served as a partial distraction.

Denita, meanwhile, was trying to cope with everyday life at home. Her anguish was intensified by the fact that she had to see Anderson's bedroom and even go into his bedroom from time to time. During one of these visits to his bedroom, to retrieve something from a closet, she suddenly heard a voice in her head that said, "Denita, look under the mattress!" She walked over to Anderson's bed, pulled up one side of the mattress, and looked to see if something was lodged between the mattress and box springs. There was nothing. This happened on Tuesday, the day after Anderson left. The following morning, Denita was again in his room and she heard the voice repeat, "Denita, look under the mattress!" This time she went to the other side of the mattress, lifted it up, and again saw nothing. Later that day, she was in Anderson's room again when the voice once more said, "Denita, look under the mattress!"

At the time, we were not sure whether it was God talking to her or one of His angels, but I have since come to believe this was the

Holy Spirit giving a word of knowledge to Denita as described in 1 Corinthians 12:8. (I am convinced she routinely receives such words from the Holy Spirit. I just never knew what to call it in the past.) The third time Denita heard the voice, she thought to herself, *Oh, this is ridiculous!* She walked over to the bed and with all her strength heaved the mattress up as far as it would go. There, in the exact center of the bed, was a folder. It could not be seen by raising the mattress on either side as she had done before.

The contents of the folder were very upsetting, and Denita refrained from calling me at work to tell me what she had found, for fear of also upsetting me. She waited until I got home to tell me she thought we were dealing with something very, very evil. She explained to me how she had come to find the folder she was holding in her hands, and then she let me examine the contents. The first thing I saw was a photograph of Mary and two other people. In this photograph, Mary was looking straight into the camera, and she had the worst case of redeye I have ever seen in a photo. That, combined with the expression on her face, made her look very evil. But it wasn't just the effects of the photo that made her look evil. There also was a handwritten letter from Mary to Anderson that had been written in Theban, an ancient alphabet associated with occultic practices such as witchcraft. Along with the letter was a key that related Theban characters to characters in our alphabet. But it was not necessary for us to translate the letter because it had already been translated and written down by Anderson. I will not relate to you the contents of the letter, but its contents, combined with the sinister-looking photo of Mary, delivered a very dark message. Mary and Anderson were connected by a bond that went beyond the emotional and physical and into the dark world of occultism.

After Denita first examined the contents of the folder, she recalled one recent day when Anderson had come downstairs and asked her, somewhat out of the blue, "Do you know how people always say that our alphabet came from the Greek alphabet? Well, it doesn't come from Greek, it comes from Theban." He explained that Theban was a language older than Greek, and that the Greek alphabet was actually descended from Theban. In hindsight, Anderson dropped many clues that he was involved in occultic activities, but we were too ignorant of such things to realize what was happening. Our religious background and our studies had formed the belief in our minds that things like witchcraft, sorcery, and summoning up the dead were never real. I actually believed they were only condemned in the Bible because believing in such practices, even if they weren't real, took away from God's glory.

The contents of the folder multiplied the pain we already felt, and that night, instead of conducting our normal Wednesday evening Bible study, we asked our small congregation to conduct a special prayer service for our family. We had already determined that we would call our friend Bootsie later that evening, so as soon as we got home we gave her a call. We wanted to call Bootsie because we now had almost no doubts that we were dealing with a case of demon possession, and Bootsie was the only person we knew who had once had a demon herself and had been delivered from it.

The conversation with Bootsie was almost surreal to me, because she was so perceptive and seemed to have such a grasp on something I knew nothing about. It was almost like she knew what we were going to tell her before we told her. The conversation began with Denita telling Bootsie, "We have reason to believe that Anderson is demon-possessed. We called you because you are the only person we know who has had a demon."

Bootie's reply took us back: "And it also just so happens that you've called somebody whose brother is an exorcist." She went on to explain how her brother, Doug Mann, was one of the ministers at Belmont Church in Nashville. He had once been delivered from a demon himself, and for the last thirty years or so he had cast demons out of many people through the power of Christ. At this point, I was beginning to wonder what kind of silliness we were getting into, but as the conversation progressed, I became more comfortable, and I realized from what Bootsie was telling us that she really knew what she was talking about.

As Denita described to Bootsie the events that led us to believe Anderson was demon-possessed, she would intervene and, without even taking time to think, offer an explanation of the things that had happened. For example, when Denita explained to Bootsie about this "Han" spirit Anderson talked to, Bootsie immediately said,

"That's his familiar spirit." Well, neither Denita nor I knew anything about familiar spirits, but Bootsie sure did. She explained to us how familiar spirits make themselves appear as friends when they are actually deceiving spirits who cause people to see or think things that are false.

I would learn later that when people seek to make contact with a deceased loved one through a medium, oftentimes a spirit that looks and sounds like the deceased person actually appears. But what really appears in these cases is a familiar spirit. In Anderson's case, the familiar spirit was there to help him see other spirits and to give him the false notion that he had power against those spirits. It also helped him have the ability, with the help of "good spirits," which were actually evil spirits themselves, to keep demons away from himself and from others. Bootsie told us that the familiar spirit was the demon possessing Anderson, and she told us matter-of-factly that it needed to be cast out. She explained these things to us in a way that made it sound as though this was all common knowledge, but it sure wasn't any knowledge we had.

After Denita finished going through the whole story with Bootsie, we asked her to relate her own experiences with demon possession. Denita had heard the story, and she had told it to me, but I had never heard it firsthand. Bootsie had suffered from deep depression, alcoholism, and prescription drug abuse in her younger years, and she was completely devoid of joy and hope. She told us about how she had watched an Episcopal priest cast a demon out of another woman, causing her to throw up in a bucket. Bootsie said she didn't really understand what was happening at this point. Instead of being scared by this sight, she just thought to herself that this was a strange way to minister to someone. Bootsie then told us how the priest walked over to her and began to exorcise her demons. She began to cackle loudly like a witch. The priest asked her what she felt, and she said, "Hate." He commanded the demon of hate to come out of her in the name of Jesus. But Bootsie had more than one demon, so the priest continued the exorcism.

At some point Bootsie attained superhuman strength and pushed the priest across the room by butting him with her shoulder. She described to us how the priest laid his hands on her and commanded the demons to come out of her, and immediately a feeling of peace she had never known before washed over her. That sense of peace has never left her. There is no doubt in Bootsie's mind that she had a demon, or demons, and I have no reason to doubt her. Bootsie is not the kind of woman who would make up stories or embellish the truth, especially where spiritual matters are concerned.

By the end of the conversation with Bootsie, she had convinced us we needed to talk to her brother, and she ended the conversation by praying for Anderson. She explained to us she would not try to cast out the demons, because she wasn't sure if she could do that without Anderson being present. Instead, she prayed for the "binding" of the demons until such point that they could actually be cast out. In her prayer she commanded in the name of Jesus Christ that the demons be bound and cease from acting upon Anderson.

Denita and I found out later that immediately after our discussion with Bootsie, she called her brother and discussed our situation with him. She stayed up for several hours praying for us, particularly Anderson. I don't think I have ever received that much prayer all at one time from any one person in my life. And not only did Bootsie pray for us, but Doug did too. The following afternoon, Denita called Doug to schedule a time for the two of us to call him and discuss everything with him. Doug decided to offer as much help as he could right then, and for about an hour they discussed Anderson's situation. Doug spent a lot of time trying to convince Denita that demon possession really does occur today, even though many of our religious traditions don't allow for it, and all Christians have the ability today to cast out demons in the name of Christ. It did not take a lot of convincing on Doug's part. By this time, we were both convinced Anderson was somehow possessed, or at least influenced by a demon or demons, so when Doug explained what should be done about it, his words fell upon receptive ears.

I was at work when Denita and Doug talked, but following the conversation, Denita called to fill me in on what she and Doug had discussed. Denita was amazed I had been able to go to work at all that week. I must admit it was difficult, because I thought about Anderson so much, and I felt like I had lost him. But things were very busy at work, and the activity forced me to focus on things other than Anderson. Fortunately, I have the kind of job where I can break away and have a private phone conversation if necessary. So Denita called and explained how Doug emphasized to her that what Jesus said in Mark 16:17—"and these signs will follow those who believe: In My name they will cast out demons . . ."—is still in effect and applies to all Christians. Doug explained to Denita that we needed to command the demons in the name of Jesus Christ to leave Anderson and to not return. He told her we needed to use the authority God had given us. He emphasized to her that we should not ask God to cast out the demons, but we should command the demons ourselves.

Well, I had some doubts about whether or not I really had this authority, because of the rest of the sentence that begins in Mark 16:17: ". . . They will speak with new tongues; they will take up serpents, and if they drink anything deadly it will by no means hurt them, they will lay hands on the sick, and they will recover." I believed such things as demon possession, casting out demons, and miraculous healing through the laying on of hands had all gone away once the church was well established and the apostles were no longer around to pass miraculous gifts along to Christians. But I was desperate, and I believed Anderson was being attacked somehow by Satan, and I felt like there must be some way to fight back. So as I was driving home that afternoon I prayed to God and asked Him to help me. I felt a boldness against Satan building up within me. I said my own version of the words Doug told Denita we should say when we attempted to cast the demons out of Anderson: "I command you demons in the name of Jesus Christ to come out of Anderson and to never return! I command you in the name of Jesus Christ to leave him and never bother him again!"

That evening Denita and I went to visit my parents because they didn't know what had been going on with Anderson. I did most of the talking and explained to them in as much detail as I could everything that had happened. We showed them some of Anderson's artwork. He is an excellent artist and spent much of his spare time making extremely detailed pencil drawings. Many of his drawings followed a fantasy theme. There were monsters, elves, swords, knives, and dragons. He was particularly fond of dragons. I had not noticed anything particularly sinister about these drawings until I reached the conclusion that Anderson was under demonic influences. He drew such things as creatures that were part human with horns on their heads brandishing swords, their faces twisted into distorted expressions. Satan had done a good job of deceiving me into thinking such drawings were harmless. My parents agreed that these drawings were troubling. Then we showed them the contents of the folder Denita found under Anderson's mattress. After hearing all the facts, my parents were convinced that Anderson had a serious problem, but I could tell they were not convinced the problem was demons. My dad led us all in prayer and asked God to take away the things Anderson was seeing and to otherwise help him.

During the conversation with my parents, my youngest brother, Lance, who lived just a few blocks away from my parents, called to talk to my dad. He said Anderson had just called his house and left a message asking if he could spend the night. As my brother did not know anything about what had been happening, he called my dad to find out if he knew why Anderson might want to spend the night there. My dad quickly explained the situation to Lance and then said he wanted to try to get Anderson to come see his grandparents. My dad called Anderson right after that and convinced him to come to their house. Anderson said he had found a place to stay that night so he wouldn't be staying with my brother, but he would come see them the next day. This was Thursday night, and we had not heard from Anderson since Monday night. We had no idea where he had been staying.

CHAPTER 7

Studying Scripture in a New Light

W hen Denita talked to Doug Mann, he promised to e-mail us a document he had written on demon possession and deliverance. We received the text he had promised later that day. I was off from work the next day, so Denita and I spent the entire morning on our front porch studying the things Doug had written and the numerous Bible passages he referenced, including Mark 16:17-18. We read passages in a different way than we ever had before.

One of the things that intrigued me was what Doug had to say about generational curses in his study on deliverance. This helped me to understand how it was possible that Anderson could have come under the influence of demons as an innocent child. I realized as I studied Doug's material, and later as I studied the works of men like Dr. Koch, that there is a very strong link between occultic practices or other sinful behavior by a person in one generation and demonic bondage inflicted upon family members generations later.

For the first time, I considered that Numbers 14:18 might be a general statement about God's wrath and the consequences of sin rather than something that held true only in that day and age in which the passage was written: "The Lord is longsuffering and abundant in mercy, forgiving iniquity and transgression; but He by no means clears the guilty, visiting the iniquity of the fathers on the children to the third and fourth generation."

I didn't have to study the material Doug sent us for very long to become convinced that we were battling demons, that Anderson was being manipulated by a deceptive familiar spirit, and that we had the weapons to fight back. So with total conviction, Denita and I prayed what I am sure was the most fervent prayer we had ever prayed together. We praised God and asked Him for His help. I again commanded the demons in the name of Jesus to come out of Anderson and never return. Then a most remarkable thing happened. Not even a minute after finishing the prayer, our telephone rang. It was my mother. She called to tell us that Anderson was on his way to their house when his car broke down just a few blocks away. She told us he was fine and his grandpa had gone to help him.

After I hung up the phone and told Denita what had happened, she exclaimed, "Praise God! He's made his car break down!" One of the things for which we had been praying was that God would somehow humble Anderson. Well, here it was, and not only would this humble him, but we both felt like his grandparents now had a captive audience. We had been afraid that if Anderson didn't like what they had to say to him he would just leave. Now he had to stay, at least for a while.

Later that afternoon my mother called to tell us the alternator was the problem with the car and that it was being replaced. Anderson later told us the man who replaced it, a longtime friend of the family, said in all his years of working with alternators he had never seen one blow apart like the one in Anderson's car. He said all of the screws inside the alternator had come completely out and the windings had come apart. We knew God had done that! That evening Anderson called and asked if he could come home. Of course, we said yes! We had never felt such joy in our lives.

I felt like the father in the Bible who welcomed home his prodigal son. Denita, Anderson, and I sat down on the front porch to talk. We were so anxious to find out if he still had demons. I did not tell him about the revelation God had brought upon us the last few days. Instead, I asked Anderson if he could still see spirits or was still being bothered by them. Anderson looked at us with a strange, bewildered expression on his face and said, "No, I haven't been able to see anything since late yesterday." You could have knocked us over with a feather! At that point, the whole world changed for me. I remember remarking several times, "Things don't work the way I thought they did." I also remember being in such a state of amazement that I felt like I had gotten out of bed one morning to find that the sun had turned blue, water was running uphill, and people could fly by merely flapping their arms. I felt as though I had to rethink everything I thought I knew.

Later, Anderson told us that it was either late Thursday night or very early Friday morning when it happened. I had prayed for him at around 5 p.m. the previous day, and his grandpa had led us in prayer for him at about 9 p.m. I don't know when Bootsie or Doug might have offered prayers on Anderson's behalf, although I know they prayed a lot. Bootsie stayed up most of the night praying after our conversation with her on Wednesday. I suspect there was a slight delay in the prayers being answered because God waited for a time when Anderson was involved in doing something in which he would notice God's intervention, like astral traveling or battling demons, because Anderson also told us later that he was "in the middle of doing something" and all of a sudden "he couldn't do it anymore."

Anderson was very surprised as we told him about the events that had taken place while he was gone. We explained to him the whole series of events from the day he left home. He seemed surprised by the fact that we could interfere with his "seeing things." Now that we felt assured Anderson was not being influenced by demons, we had a conversation with him about his past behavior, since he had previously expressed to us his belief that he had done some things for which he couldn't be forgiven. He opened up on several points, but he still withheld some things from us, as we would later learn.

Anderson confessed to us he had been involved in some illegal activities, including owning and operating a street racing team. He attained this status by out-racing all other members of the team. He became involved in street racing after a co-worker invited him to some racing events. Sometimes I wonder how my son was able to accomplish this without my having any idea about what was taking place, and then I remind myself that he usually worked at night, and very often would call home to tell us he had to work extra hours for some reason or another.

For those who might not know anything about it, street racing really amounts to nothing more than gangs driving fast cars. The young men and women who are involved in this activity are seeking thrills and living on the wrong side of the law. I was surprised to learn from Anderson that street racing is an underworld unto itself. Many street racers also serve as couriers for the delivery of illegal drugs. Many make a game out of delivering a supply of drugs faster than another driver. Not surprisingly, street racers carry weapons with them, and Anderson was supplied with one himself. He told us he had had a gun pointed in his face by somebody who had just lost a race with him and didn't want to pay the agreed upon amount of money. He had responded by pointing his own pistol at the other guy, who backed down and paid Anderson his winnings.

Anderson told us later that he had actually used his pistol against others and easily could have killed some people, but by the grace of God he never did. It is still very hard for me to believe that my son could ever have been so cold, hard, and mean. I also know that many children are able to fool their parents, but I never thought of myself as that easily fooled. Yet it happened, and I urge parents who read this to take heed. No matter how good a parent you think you are, some things are just out of your control. And I urge you to never judge any parent whose child gets into trouble. Instead pray for them and help them through the pain. I'm telling you, the pain is tremendous.

The positive side of this story is that Anderson assured us he was leaving that kind of life behind. However, we knew and he knew there could still be serious consequences as a result of his actions. Of all the things Anderson experienced while living his life of crime, one in particular had a very marked effect on him emotionally. He told us how he saw the police corner a friend of his and shoot him dead. Anderson was waiting to meet this friend and so was out of sight when it happened. He was very angry at the policeman who shot his friend because the friend had not pulled a gun on the policeman. As I listened to Anderson tell me all these things, I began to wonder whether Anderson should turn himself in to the police. I decided to wait and let God take care of that one. And take care of it He did. Later in the story, you will see how all of this was resolved. The Lord was so merciful to Anderson and the rest of us in so many ways. Anderson could have very easily ended up dead or in prison as a result of his sins, but God spared Him.

As we continued our discussion with Anderson, he confessed he had taken up smoking. He claimed he was able to quit whenever he wanted to, and that he actually had quit. We would find out later that he might have quit, but only temporarily. Anderson described in detail the activities in which he had been involved. He said he had asked God to forgive him. But he still didn't tell us what it was he had done at school that was so bad. That would come later.

Our happiness over Anderson's return home and his seemingly more docile condition was short-lived as we soon discovered there was a spiritual emptiness in his life. He was extremely quiet and introspective. We asked him what was wrong and he said he felt like he had lost a friend or something very familiar to him. He said he had a big void in his life now. He even said he didn't know what to think about. His mind seemed empty now whereas before he had spent so much time and mental energy interacting with spirits and battling the demons he encountered.

Anderson never seemed remorseful about his previous behavior. The only wrong he acknowledged committing was "jumping the gun" on moving out of the house. We talked with him at length about how he needed Jesus to fill the void in his heart. We also warned him about the words of Jesus in Matthew 12:43-45: "When an unclean spirit goes out of a man, he goes through dry places, seeking rest, and finds none. Then he says, 'I will return to my house from which I came.' And when he comes he finds it empty, swept, and put in order. Then he goes and takes with him seven other spirits more wicked than himself, and they enter and dwell there; and the last state of that man is worse than the first. So shall it be with this wicked generation." Sadly, Anderson had yet to give God praise for his deliverance.

There are three primary reasons why I believe, beyond any shadow of a doubt, Anderson really was seeing spirits, really had demonic influences, and really was delivered by God. First of all was his admission that he suddenly "quit seeing things (spirits)." Second, the strange, bewildered look he now had due to losing his ability to see spirits continued for several days. He walked around as if he had lost something or somebody very important and seemed to be at a loss for what to do about it. The last thing that convinces me Anderson was delivered is the complete change we saw in his sleep habits over the next few nights. During the previous four years he had only slept a few hours each night, sometimes as few as two or three hours. He had tried various sleep aids, but nothing worked. Now he was going to bed early and sleeping all night. He would sleep late sometimes. Even he commented on the change.

When Anderson came home, he announced he wanted to quit school. We thought this was very strange because he was pursuing a career he had longed for and prepared for since early high school. He realized this meant he had to find a full-time job because we weren't going to let him sit around the house and do nothing, so he began looking for full-time work. Over the course of the next few days we learned that Anderson had very little faith. He said he believed there was a God who created the world, but he wasn't sure the Bible was the inspired Word of God or that Jesus was the Son of God. That was a tremendous blow to us. After all the years of teaching at home and in the church, how could he doubt? But we would not despair, and we only assumed we had some work cut out for us. I ordered books and DVDs to help me better understand how to help Anderson find the answers to his questions.

During this time, Denita began having troubling episodes in which a vile and vulgar word entered her mind suddenly and involuntarily. This was a word she had never spoken and which had never before entered her mind in such a way. This happened only occasionally at first, but as time went on it happened more and more frequently, and it was very upsetting to her. She could not even study her Bible or pray without the word entering her mind. In fact, the problem seemed to be at its worst when she tried to read her Bible, and the problem reached its peak during the week that Anderson was away from home. Denita prayed constantly to be delivered from this malady, and we prayed together often, commanding the demon that was putting those thoughts in her mind to leave her alone.

Gradually, the word stopped coming into Denita's mind, but for several weeks this was a very serious problem for her that brought her to tears many times. We concluded that it was more than just a coincidence that this happened at the same time we were spending so much time in prayer for Anderson. It seemed to us that Satan was trying to diminish Denita's ability to fight for her son.

After all the stress we had been through we decided we all needed a vacation, so we went to Orange Beach, Alabama, the next week for a few days. During this time, I reviewed some of the material I had ordered. I hoped that when we returned home Anderson and I would spend some time discussing the evidences that God is who He claims to be in the Bible and that the Bible actually is God's inspired Word. However, I never had the opportunity to have those discussions with Anderson. He was not interested in talking about anything, particularly spiritual matters, and he became increasingly distant. He didn't seem to be with us mentally, and Denita and I were very concerned about him. He didn't appear to care about his spiritual well-being. It seemed to us that he had not gone through much of a transformation after his return home, and it bothered us that he was not glorifying God for his deliverance from demons.

CHAPTER 8

A Demon in the Car

S hortly after returning home from the beach, on the evening of
the first day of May, Denita decided to have a talk with
Anderson to try to understand what was going on in his head. She
wanted to know whether or not he was concerned about his spiritual
state. After a long discussion on the subject, she decided I needed to
be involved in the conversation. She was concerned because
Anderson was again expressing his lack of faith and exhibiting
signs of demonic influence or possession.

During the few days since Denita's conversation with Doug, we
both had read a copy of a book he recommended. The book is titled
Deliver Us From Evil,[1] written by Don Basham, a Disciples of
Christ minister. More than once Basham found himself in a position
where God instructed him to cast demons out of people. Having read
this book, the book by Dr. Koch on demonology, and the material
Doug sent us, I felt prepared for what happened next. Anderson
became more and more agitated as we discussed God, Christ, and
Satan, and God's love for us. We also discussed the war going on
between God and Satan. Anderson obstinately refused to see that
God had done anything for him. He said things like: "How do I
know Satan didn't take away my ability to see things just to make us
think God did it? Why does God let bad things happen to people? It
doesn't make any sense! Why does God allow us to do bad things

and then send us to hell for it? It's all just a game for God!"

I tried my best to convince Anderson that God gives us the choice to obey or disobey Him, because He wants true love from us, and that true love can only occur when we have the choice to not love. It was like he wasn't even hearing me. "But it doesn't make sense! Why didn't God create us so that we have to love Him?" I felt like I was having a conversation with somebody I had never met before.

Denita asked Anderson if there were any people in his past he needed to forgive for anything they had done to him. We had read that forgiveness sometimes is the key to loosening the hold a demon has on a person, so we thought we would give it a try. He did admit harboring anger toward a couple of people, one of which was the guy Anderson had beaten up. The other one was the policeman who had shot Anderson's friend.

When I said something to Anderson that indicated I believed he wanted to forgive this policeman, he became furious and said, "I never said I wanted to forgive him!" So we abandoned that particular topic of discussion, but not without first explaining to Anderson the dangers of harboring such intense anger. As Anderson became more animated and belligerent in his arguments, his eyes seemed to roll back in his head, and I remember having that thought again that Anderson could just go berserk at a time like this and try to kill us. Once again I dismissed the thought and trusted God to take care of us. Denita said later that Anderson's eyes became completely dilated during this conversation. Mothers always notice everything about their children, and dads are so oblivious. Denita and I thought that maybe all of Anderson's demons had not been cast out. He allowed me to attempt to cast any remaining demons out of him, but nothing happened. Knowing what I know now, I can say with confidence he was once again "seeing things" at this point, and he was possessed, but my prayers were ineffective because he was resisting.

The following days proved to be even more stressful. Anderson became increasingly belligerent. He asked if he could stop attending church because he felt like a hypocrite. The rule in our house had always been that anyone who lived under our roof went to church. We realized we couldn't force this on someone who didn't want to live the Christian life. We told him that he couldn't continue conducting himself in such a manner and live in our house. During this time he was also staying out very late and not letting us know where he was or what he was doing. When he was at home he stayed in his room with the door closed. We agreed to let him remain at home until he could find a full-time job. We felt like he was only half-heartedly looking for work. Because of this we stayed on his case constantly, reminding him that he only had a short time to find work before we kicked him out.

One morning, Anderson slept extremely late and Denita was irritated because he hadn't left to look for work. She went to his room to make him get up, and when she opened his door he looked as if he were dead. She shook him for a long time before he finally moved. When he did, she saw bloody gashes on his left shoulder. She knew instantly he had done this to himself because she had seen marks similar to this on him about a week before, but they were not nearly as bad as these marks. When she had asked him about those marks he said he got them accidentally while looking for something in the barn. She knew at the time he was lying, but she chose not to press him for the truth. Denita sat down on the side of the bed and, taking Anderson's hand in her own, asked him if he had self-mutilated. He admitted he had.

Denita and I both discussed this self-mutilation problem with Anderson, and he seemed to be convinced it really was a problem and that he needed some kind of help. Denita once again contacted Doug asking for a recommendation on a good Christian counselor for Anderson. Through his personal contacts in Nashville, Doug, within hours, managed to get Anderson's story not only to a Christian psychologist in Birmingham, but also to a Christian psychiatrist with whom he shared a practice. The psychiatrist was not taking new patients at the time, but remarkably she agreed to take Anderson right away. Again, we were humbled and amazed at the way God worked with lightning speed to help us. This time, however, the help could not be rendered. But it wasn't God's fault.

A few days later, on May 22, Anderson and Mary went water skiing with my brother Lance, my sister-in-law, my nephew, and my nephew's girlfriend. That evening, just as it became dark, Victoria and I were playing a board game when we heard Anderson's car pull up outside. I expected Anderson and Mary to come through the front door when I heard them walking on the porch, but instead there was a knock on the door. Victoria went to open the door, and what a sight met us! Anderson stumbled through the front door with his arm around Mary. She had to support him because he could not walk under his own power. He had a look of anguish on his face, and he was groaning so that I thought he had been injured in some way. I noticed right away the two of them were sunburned and wondered if maybe that was causing him pain. But as all of these thoughts were going through my head, Mary said, "One of the demons attacked him again."

My heart sank. "Oh, no. Oh, no," I said. I helped Mary get Anderson to the sofa while Victoria looked on in shock and fear. Anderson had to struggle to speak, but he and Mary did manage to tell me that he had fallen asleep on the sofa at my brother's house, and the demon came to him in his dreams. Later, my brother said Mary became scared because of the noises Anderson was making in his sleep, so she made him wake up. Lance told me that Anderson looked like somebody on drugs when he came out of that sleep, and he acted very strange. As my brother still was not aware of all that had happened with Anderson, he was a little perplexed by all of this. He was sure that, whatever the problem was, Anderson was in no shape to be driving, so he convinced Mary to drive the two of them home. It was then that the demon attack intensified. Anderson said the demon was in the back of his car and made his arms and legs numb to the point that he could not use them. This was why he could barely walk.

Once we got Anderson to the sofa, I sat down next to him and asked him, "What is in you?"

Anderson replied, as if in pain, "There's nothing in me. They don't have to be in you to do things to you."

I immediately prayed over Anderson and commanded the demon to leave him, but nothing noticeable happened right away. Gradually, over the next ten minutes or so, his discomfort diminished and he regained the use of his arms and legs.

When Anderson and Mary first arrived, Denita was in the shower. I went to tell her what was happening and she hurriedly ended her shower and came to the living room. The first thing she did when she saw Anderson was attempt to remove his necklace. The pendant on the necklace depicted a dragon holding up a pentagram with its wings. It was similar to one given to him by the teacher at school who was a shaman. Denita had thrown that one away when he came back home the first time. Anderson wouldn't let his mom remove the necklace, and Mary pleaded with her not to remove it because it was his protection against the demons. Mary and Anderson both said the necklace got hot during the demon attack in the car, as if this was supposed to convince us that the necklace was helping him. But it was clear to us that Anderson wasn't receiving any help from anything at that point.

Once I got over the initial shock and I could see that Anderson was feeling better, I began to feel anger toward Satan and this demon that was attacking my son. I was ready to do battle, whatever it took. I asked Anderson if the demon was still in his car. He said that it was, and I asked him how he knew. He replied that he just knew it was there. I said, "Let's go out there."

Anderson followed me, and we went to his car. I asked him, "Where is it?" He said it was where the back seat should be, as he had removed his back seat to make room for stereo equipment. I opened that door and said, "Is it there?" Anderson replied that it was. I began to command with all my might in the name of Jesus that the demon leave. While I was doing this, Anderson leaned over and rested his arms and head on the trunk of the car. He still seemed tired and weak.

After praying, I said, "Is it still there?" It was. I noticed that Anderson was still wearing the necklace and told him to remove it. He did, but he continued to hold it in his hand. I prayed some more, commanding the demon to leave. Then I asked again, "Is it still there?"

"Yes."

"What is it doing?"

"It's just sitting there, looking at you."

"Is it right here?" I put my hand into the car, in the space the demon should be occupying.

"Yeah. Your hand is in it."

"Can you tell me what it looks like?"

"It looks like a little Buddha, about two feet tall, and it's sitting there with its legs crossed and its hands between its legs."

I was becoming frustrated that I could not make the demon go away, and then I remembered reading that demons usually can't be cast out unless the oppressed or possessed person wants to be delivered. I asked Anderson, "Do you want these spirits to be gone?"

He replied, "Yeah, this one." I gave up and we went into the house. I asked Denita to go out onto the front porch with me so that I could tell her in private what had transpired. When we went back inside, Anderson's words finally sank in. I asked him what he had meant when he said "this one." When Denita heard that, she immediately knew that this was not just an unexpected demonic attack, but that Anderson had been seeing the spirits again for quite a while and had invited them back after God made them go away. When we asked him if that was so, he said it was. We both became angry at that point. We did not yell at them, but we were angry that these two young people were engaging in such sinful and dangerous behavior.

I learned later that while Anderson and I were outside, Denita and Mary were having a not-so-pleasant conversation of their own. Anderson and Mary had already told me that Anderson was caught off guard by this demon because he wasn't expecting it. Mary told Denita that Anderson was angry with us because we had taken away his ability to fight the demons. Anderson and Mary said they had to constantly be on guard to fight the demons. Denita asked Mary why they would want to live the kind of life where they had to constantly be on guard against demons. Why would they not want to turn to God and let Him remove that from their lives? Mary responded by making hateful remarks about God, Christianity, and Denita.

I also found out later that while Denita and I were outside together discussing what had transpired at Anderson's car, Mary and Anderson laughed about the fact that I was unable to make the demon leave. They also thought I was angry because it wouldn't leave. I was angry, as I already said, but not because I couldn't make that demon leave. I was very frustrated about the whole situation, and I now know that the demon couldn't be cast out, even in the name of Jesus, because Anderson did not want to be delivered. He just wanted the "bad" spirits to go away. He didn't realize they were all bad spirits.

Once we found out Anderson was actively participating in the occult again, Denita and I decided it was time for drastic action. We told Mary to call her parents to pick her up and take her home. But before that, I pleaded with Mary and Anderson to turn away from this evil activity. I read to them God's instruction to Israel in Deuteronomy 18:9-12:

> When you come into the land which the Lord your God is giving you, you shall not learn to follow the abominations of those nations. There shall not be found among you anyone who makes his son or his daughter pass through the fire, or one who practices witchcraft, or a soothsayer, or one who interprets omens, or a sorcerer, or one who conjures spells, or a medium, or a spiritist, or one who calls up the dead. For all who do these things are an abomination to the Lord, and because of these abominations the Lord your God drives them out from before you.

Before our family had these terrible experiences, this passage had very little meaning for me. In fact, I hardly noticed it was in the Bible at all. I credit Doug Mann with my new appreciation of the stark warnings of this passage. I know now that my son basically had the abilities of a medium and that those abilities only come from Satan, never from God. We told Anderson that ours was a Christian home, and he was no longer welcome as long as he continued in occultic practices. During our very emotionally charged conversation with him, his eyes became completely dilated just as they had that night in his bedroom.

After Mary was gone, we gave Anderson enough money in the form of two checks that he would be able to rent an apartment for several months while he looked for a job. We told him we still loved him and sent him on his way. It was very hard to do that, knowing there was a demon in his car, but we felt we had no choice. One of our primary concerns was Victoria's well being. All the turmoil surrounding Anderson had detracted from our relationship with her, and I knew she was probably scared by all of these things. We felt better when we learned my parents had taken Anderson into their home, and part of the comfort we felt came from the knowledge that he had not completely distanced himself from his family.

The usual reaction to this story is, well, there just has to be some explanation for all these things other than demonic activity. Demon possession and casting out demons are things we read about in the Bible, but that doesn't happen today! Anderson must have some kind of mental illness, or he must have fallen in with some kind of cult and been brainwashed or given some kind of mind-altering drug. There was a time when I would have reacted exactly the same way, but not now. I have been face to face with occultism, and I am convinced that it is condemned in God's Word. I believe this not just because practicing it shows a lack of faith in God and indicates a desire to seek answers elsewhere, as I used to believe, but also because Satan does grant the ability to contact his spirits. Those who serve as mediums and practice witchcraft actually can have supernatural abilities, although this is not always the case.

My usual response to someone who doubts Anderson ever actually saw spirits is this: "If this was just some sort of mental illness that caused him to think he was seeing spirits, why did God make it go away after our prayers, only to allow it to return? What would be gained by God healing somebody only to allow their disease to return? And what is the explanation for the voice Denita heard on three separate occasions imploring her to look under Anderson's mattress, and for the startling result when she finally obeyed the voice? Should we conclude that Denita too has a mental illness that causes her to hear voices in her head, and that finding the folder under Anderson's mattress was just a coincidence?"

I am now convinced there are very few coincidences in life. We probably make God angry by attributing way too many things to coincidence, or chance, or luck, instead of giving Him the glory. In my mind, the much more plausible explanation for what happened to Anderson is that he had the satanic ability to see spirits and to communicate with them. His ability was lost through our prayers but regained when he refused to allow Christ to become Master of his life and the Holy Spirit to replace the evil spirits.

CHAPTER 9

Victoria's Nightmares

About a month or so after Anderson left our home and moved in with my parents, Victoria came to her mom with some information that should have been brought to our attention much sooner, but we understood why she was reluctant to tell us. After a discussion with Victoria, Denita told me what Victoria was too embarrassed to tell me herself. She said for some time Victoria had been having nightmares about being raped. She usually couldn't see who was raping her in these dreams, but sometimes she said there was a "dark form" there. The most troubling thing about these nightmares was that upon waking, Victoria would feel pain in areas of her body where a girl or woman might expect to feel pain after having undergone such a heinous attack.

To make things even more interesting, the nightmares had increased in frequency since Anderson moved out of the house. I did not want to interpret this as demonic activity, but I also could not ignore the very real possibility that it was. I tried to reason that Victoria was having these nightmares because her subconscious mind was trying to cope with the trauma of the recent months. But what about the pain? Did she have some physical problem that was causing the pain, and the nightmares were the result? I know that sometimes happens to me. I will put my arm into an uncomfortable position in my sleep and have a dream about my arm hurting as a result. But I've never had such dreams in a recurring pattern. Denita and I decided this was likely another attack by Satan upon our family, and we decided to counterattack. If a prayer of deliverance didn't solve the problem, then we would seek medical help.

That same night, before Victoria went to bed, Denita and I laid our hands on Victoria and we all prayed together. In the name of Jesus I commanded the demon that was visiting Victoria in her sleep and causing those nightmares to leave her and never return. We never had to seek medical help as Victoria never had the nightmare, or the pain, again. We continued to pray with Victoria every night for about a week, calling upon God to protect her in her sleep with the blood of Christ, and after that, she began to pray that prayer every night by herself.

I do not expect everyone who reads this to believe this was another case of demons being cast out in the name of Jesus. Not so long ago, I would have reasoned that all that happened was the prayer just gave Victoria reassurance that everything was going to be fine; her subconscious was appeased and decided it did not need to deal with this issue any longer. As in the case of Anderson's temporary deliverance, there is an important reason—and a very compelling reason—why this really was demonic activity. After Anderson moved in with my parents, we continued to communicate with him, mostly by telephone, because we wanted him to understand we still loved him. Gradually, the tensions between us eased somewhat and we could have conversations with him without his displays of anger. On one such occasion, Denita told Anderson about what had happened with Victoria, and he didn't seem surprised at all by what he was told. He told his mom he was certain those nightmares were demonic. He said normal people don't have recurring nightmares, only those who are influenced by demons. He said that Mary had gone through exactly the same thing. She had the same recurring nightmare and the same pain.

Anderson said that Mary's parents had taken her to doctors, including a psychiatrist, to find out what her problem was, but no doctor could find anything wrong with her, physically or mentally. It is more than just interesting to me that Victoria had never had these nightmares until she met Mary. The fact that the nightmares started at about the same time Victoria met Mary and intensified after Anderson left the house, and that Mary had had the same kind of nightmare, convinces me the nightmares were the result of demonic influence that was somehow connected to Mary. Did Victoria get this demon from Mary? I don't know the answer for certain, but it seems insufficient to call this a coincidence.

Not long after our prayers for Victoria, Denita experienced a magnificent display of God's power in her life. To understand this event, some background information is in order. Denita had suffered from fibromyalgia and rheumatoid arthritis for many years. Eight years earlier the pain and fatigue had become so bad she spent most afternoons on the sofa or in bed. Her health improved after she began taking all-natural dietary supplements. She chose this method of treatment because doctors had found no solution to her problems. For several years her pain was significantly diminished and her energy level increased through the use of supplements. However, her pain and fatigue slowly returned until they became significant enough to once again seriously affect her quality of life.

On July 26, while working at the kitchen sink, Denita was in so much pain she cried out to God in tears to heal her and take away the pain. She told Him that she could not go on much longer without being confined to the bed again. She begged for healing so that she could take care of her family and continue to serve Him. God answered her prayer and healed her. About an hour after her prayer, Denita noticed the pain was gone. It had gradually gone away, and it took her that long to notice it. In fact, it all happened so subtly that she did not even realize at first that God had answered her prayer. It wasn't until three days later that she realized she had been free of pain and fatigue since the hour she prayed. At the time of this writing it has been more than eight months, and she continues to be free of pain and fatigue. We praise God every day for this miracle of healing.

This one miracle in our lives would have been enough to convince me that God still provides miraculous healing today and that we should ask Him specifically to heal us instead of just asking Him to guide the hands of the doctors who attend to us or to provide some general blessing on the sick person. Not long after Denita's healing, Denita and Victoria brought to my attention a problem Victoria had that I honestly had forgotten about in all the turmoil of those days. For quite a while, Victoria had had very bad pain in her feet, and the pain seemed to be there whether she was on her feet or not. She would even hurt while still in bed after waking up in the mornings. Denita had taken her to a doctor who fitted her with orthotics, thinking deformities in the bone structure of Victoria's feet might be the source of her problems, but these orthotics offered only minor relief.

Well, Denita and Victoria got together and decided if God could heal Denita then He could heal Victoria. I agreed, and Denita and I once again laid our hands on Victoria and this time prayed for her healing. And the result? God did it again! The pain went away almost instantly, and now Victoria only has pain in her feet after she stands on a very hard surface such as concrete for an extended period of time. Even the healthiest of feet will oftentimes suffer from that kind of treatment.

Another issue with Denita's health seemed to be related to Anderson's demonic oppression. On December 3, 2003, just a few months before Anderson revealed to us his ability to see spirits, Denita became very ill. She would have episodes where her adrenalin surged, causing her heart to race, creating nausea and weakness. Her face and neck burned constantly, and she had pain in her mouth. She even had convulsions after one episode. After several emergency room and doctor's office visits, there was no real consensus from the doctors on what condition she had, but the leading candidate seemed to be dysautonomia, a dysfunctional autonomic nervous system. However, Denita's symptoms were not like those of the classic dysautonomia patient, and she did not respond to the standard treatments. She added additional supplements to the regimen she was already taking for the fibromyalgia and arthritis. Over the next few months, her condition gradually improved, leaving her with occasional, mild episodes of increased heart rate.

We had both already reached the conclusion that Satan had launched an all-out attack upon our family, and we felt this was just another front in the battle. Denita began to wonder if perhaps this happened to her because Anderson was prepared to talk to us about his "abilities" in December. She wondered if this attack was meant to serve as a distraction to prevent him from doing so. She finally had an opportunity to ask Anderson during the summer if he had been thinking about talking to us in December. Anderson informed her that indeed he had. Remember I mentioned earlier that he had waited until he could talk to me without his mom around, for fear of upsetting her. It seems that Satan had a plan to prevent us from learning all the things we have learned, but when you have God on your side, no plan of Satan's can be successful.

CHAPTER 10

Joy at Last

D enita and I continued to talk to my parents about Anderson.
Sometimes they would call us to let us know how he was
doing, and sometimes we would call them to ask about him. There
was one such conversation we had with my parents that prompted
me to ask Anderson to come by our house so I could ask him a few
questions. My mother had mentioned something about occultic
ceremonies in which Anderson had participated and become scared
by some of the things that happened there. For example, she said he
witnessed a cross blowing up after it was placed on an altar. She
seemed to believe that Anderson was now, as a result of being
frightened, no longer engaged in occultic activity.

Through all of this, Anderson had never mentioned belonging
to any occultic group, so I wanted to find out for myself what this
was all about. He had once mentioned that he had done things at
school for which he believed he could not be forgiven. I wondered
if this had something to do with that. As for Anderson being scared
away from occultic activities, I had serious doubts. My parents still
had not come to grips with the fact that Anderson actually could see
spirits and had developed friendships with people who practiced the
occult. They preferred to believe he fell in with the wrong crowd
and was convinced by some cult that he could see spirits—and that
they even caused him to believe certain fantasies were real events in

his past life. I had never for a minute believed this was the case, but I wanted to hear from his mouth everything he had done.

Anderson agreed to come to the house one evening so I could ask him my questions. He assured us he had never joined a coven or cult, but the reasons he gave were not very comforting. He explained to us that a coven of witches or warlocks consists of seven persons, and a coven is always all male or all female. He said the reason he never joined a coven is because he could not find one that was all male and did not already have the full complement of seven members. However, he did tell us he was allowed to witness several meetings of one coven of warlocks, and he agreed to tell his mom and me about all of these instances. As it turned out, these were the events to which Anderson was referring when he told us he had done things at school for which he couldn't be forgiven, even though these events didn't actually take place at school.

The group of warlocks mentioned by Anderson consisted of seven students from the small college he was attending at the time. He had classes with a few, but not all of them. He said the way they all got to know each other was that they all had this ability to see spirits and to know when they had met another person who shared that ability. Anderson said the instant he saw each of these seven, he knew they had the ability and they knew that he had it. As I've stated before, this was done without verbal communication.

The seven warlocks invited Anderson along on several different outings after their classes were over. The first such excursion was to a cemetery where, as the story goes, an occultic ceremony took place sometime in the 1960s. Something went wrong at this ceremony, and many of the thirty members of the cult died right there in the cemetery. The ones who didn't die buried the others there and erected makeshift headstones for the graves. Some people wanted to close the cemetery after this, but a burial was scheduled there two days later. The local authorities allowed this burial to take place and then the cemetery was closed at the urging of a minister. According to the story, the deaths of these cultists were not widely published, the local authorities and family members both wishing no publicity whatever.

Anderson went with his seven friends to the cemetery to find the graves. This cemetery lies on the edge of a neighborhood that was built up around it many years ago. One more fascinating aspect of the story is that this cemetery happens to be less than a hundred yards from where Denita lived with her parents at the time I met her. She figured this out from the description Anderson gave of the cemetery and its location. Denita had never been in the cemetery, though, because it has a fence around it and the gates were locked so that no one could enter. However, Anderson did not know all of this as he described his story. His mom pointed out these details after he finished his story.

Anderson told us that people who wanted to get inside to see the mysterious graves had forced open a gate, and now it was possible to enter the cemetery through that gate. Anderson said that after a person goes through the gates in the cemetery, the gates close by themselves, but there are no springs on them. He also said that, according to the stories about this place, voices can still be heard in the vicinity of the graves of the cult members. Anderson told us that he and his friends searched for the mysterious graves and finally found them at the very back of the cemetery, in an area that didn't look like it was part of the cemetery. He said the graves were indeed there and each had a headstone with strange symbols on it, including swastikas. The graves were arranged head to head in a circular pattern. Anderson said he could hear voices as he stood there.

The second adventure Anderson told us about was when he went with his warlock friends to visit an abandoned house to try to summon spirits from it. The warlocks were dressed in their robes and other adornment and brought along their altar, upon which they burned candles and performed some of their rites. Anderson was just a bystander, but he said that as they were conjuring up the spirits, suddenly the back wall of the house became filled with spirits exiting the house. He described one of the spirits as looking exactly like a painting he saw later depicting what Count Dracula looked like when he was in his non-human form. It was not a bat; it was a monstrous-looking image.

Anderson's third adventure with his warlock acquaintances was a visit to a farmer's field just a few miles from our house, where they saw spirits without having to summon them. It was a situation similar to the one he had described to me in which spirits appeared to be wandering around aimlessly on our property in the woods. That seemed to be what was going on in this field, and Anderson and the seven warlocks could all see the spirits.

Anderson's fourth occultic adventure involved another set of acquaintances, a young man and a young woman. The three of them went to a cemetery that reportedly held a buried person who really wasn't human, but was instead a demon in physical form. Anderson said this grave looked different from other graves. Even though it had been there for several years, the dirt was still mounded up on top of it. Anderson said the other young man had brought along a crucifix, and upon arriving at the grave, he placed the crucifix into the mounded dirt. Anderson said it was impossible to keep the crucifix in the dirt. Every time it was placed into the dirt, it was forced out by some unseen hand! Finally the young man placed the crucifix on the headstone, and the crucifix exploded!

Throughout this whole ordeal, we continued to pray for the Lord's intervention, that He would touch Anderson's heart and rescue him from Satan. We continued to talk to Anderson because we wanted him to know we still loved him. We would call him on his cell phone or visit with him whenever we visited my parents. At first it was hard to know exactly how much contact to have with him because we wanted to make sure he understood that he had put up a wall between himself and us for as long as he was not willing to let the Lord deliver him from his evil spirits. We wanted to heap "coals of fire" on his head, but we also wanted to make sure he understood we loved him.

As time went on, Anderson began to contact us just to talk, and his tough, callous, and rebellious attitudes began to diminish. He found a job at an auto parts store. At first we only knew how well he was doing in his new job because my parents gave us frequent reports, but later he began to talk to us directly about his job and other topics. My mother was good about encouraging him to keep in contact with us. He started to call more and more frequently, and every time we talked to him we told him we loved him and reminded him of how important it was for him to leave Satan and let Christ rule his life. He always told us he was thinking about it.

Whenever we talked to Anderson, we urged him to consider all the things he had given up in favor of a life of sin, and he seemed to be softening. No matter what we said to him, he always wanted to talk to us, so we knew that he missed us. Finally, he was calling so frequently that his mom decided it was ridiculous that he was refusing to return to the Lord and come home. So the next time he came to the house she asked him, "You really would rather be living with us, wouldn't you?" He said that he would, and they had a very emotional heart-to-heart conversation. It was September 7, 2004, a day that will always be remembered in our family. That evening at the dinner table, Denita was relating to Victoria and me the conversation she had with Anderson when the phone rang. It was Anderson, and he wanted to come home. We all hugged each other and cried tears of joy. We prayed together, praising and thanking God, and we asked Him to bring Anderson home safely. He did bring him home safely, and after all the hugs, we sat down in the living room for some prayer.

First, because I had read many instances of where complete deliverance from occultic bondage was not possible until the person under bondage renounced any and all associations with the occult, I asked Anderson to renounce his participation in the occult. He eagerly did so and added the plea, "I want Satan to leave me alone."

Following this, I led the family in prayer and commanded Anderson's demons to leave him with the exclamation, "I cast you out in the name of Jesus Christ!" I commanded the demons to never return. This time, I believe the deliverance to be permanent, unlike the first time when Anderson was delivered without his knowledge and against his will. By the time of his deliverance, Anderson's sightings of spirits had become less frequent because he had already stopped actively using his abilities. He said that through disuse, the ability to see spirits diminishes somewhat, and I suspect that as his heart slowly turned back to the Lord, Satan's power within him began to wane. Since being delivered that night, he no longer sees spirits at all, and he doesn't self-mutilate.

I feel the need to ask a question similar to the one I asked myself following that initial, temporary deliverance: If Anderson was suffering from some kind of mental problem, why did casting out demons in the name of Jesus make it go away? Why, from that moment on, would he cease to see spirits? Why, from that moment on, would he cease to cut himself?

CHAPTER 11

Delivered From the Bondage of Witchcraft

It sounds like we should be at the end of the story, but we aren't. One of the things that was still bothering Denita and me was Anderson's continued association with Mary. He broke up with her the night he came home but later decided to continue the relationship. We knew that she was still being affected by demons and familiar spirits, and she was very hostile toward God. But God once again made His overwhelming presence felt in our lives. On September 15, seemingly out of the blue, Mary expressed her desire to be saved. Based on her confession of faith in Christ as the Son of God and her decision to accept Him as her Savior, I baptized her that afternoon according to the teachings of Mark 16:16, Matthew 28:19, and Acts 2:38.

Prior to Mary's baptism, I had commanded her demons to leave her in the name of Christ, and we thought she was free from her occultic bondage at that point. However, Denita noticed one day soon after Mary's baptism that she had cut marks on one of her hands. We knew she had a problem in the past with self-mutilation, and Anderson told us he was sure she was still cutting herself. He believed she still had a demon, which I had already surmised. Then Anderson informed us that Mary still had in her bedroom all of her books on witchcraft and magic. Mary had once been a follower of the Wiccan religion and also practiced witchcraft. She had been a so-called "white witch."

Denita and I knew those books had to be destroyed for her to be completely delivered. We also knew there was a biblical precedent, described in Acts 19:19, for burning books of magic: "Also, many of those who had practiced magic brought their books together and burned them in the sight of all." Anderson was not convinced the books needed to be destroyed. He thought it would be sufficient to throw them away, but he did agree they had to go.

On Saturday night, September 25, Anderson and Mary went to her house to box up the books and other occultic paraphernalia she had. Denita and I did not know they were doing this until we got a phone call from Anderson. He called to tell us they were on their way to our house to burn the books. We live in the country, so we have a place where we can burn tree limbs and various other discarded objects without fear of breaking any laws. Anderson's explanation for why he had decided to burn the books instead of simply putting them in the trash was that "things got a little weird" while they were boxing up the materials. He would give no more explanation than that. When Denita was convinced he was all right, she told him to remember that he could command demons to stay away in the name of Jesus. He replied, "I've already had to do that."

I went out on the front porch to wait for Anderson and Mary to arrive, and I prayed nearly the whole time for their safety. I had a very distinct feeling that they were in danger. It took about fifteen minutes for Anderson to arrive. I did not realize until then that they were traveling separately. Anderson said Mary was coming in her own car, but she had stopped to buy gas. He added that she was carrying the books and other objects in her car. I felt panic well up inside me, but I suppressed it and told Anderson maybe he should call her. He called her and asked where she was. From the end of the conversation I could hear, it sounded as though Mary might be having some problems.

Suddenly Anderson was yelling at Mary to pull off the road and into the gas station, which is just down the highway from our house. I knew something was very wrong. Anderson and I jumped into his car and sped away to the gas station to meet Mary. I wouldn't find out until later what was wrong, but Mary was being attacked somehow by something in her car. It was one or more spirits. When we got to Mary, I had her ride to our house with Anderson and I drove her car.

When we arrived, Denita met us in tears. She had been outside the house with Anderson and me when Anderson made the call to Mary, but she had gone back into the house. So when Anderson and I took off like we did, she had no idea what had happened. Denita went up to Mary and hugged her and asked if she was okay. Mary didn't reply. Her only response was to say she needed to get something out of her car.

While Denita was trying to talk with Mary, Anderson took the box of books from Mary's backseat, and he and I walked to the burn pile. Anderson asked if there were some other things we could burn. He said there were some metal objects in the box and the fire needed to be hot enough to melt them. Some other material was already waiting to be burned, so I felt like we could make a good fire.

As Anderson started to set the box on fire, Denita and Mary arrived, and Mary had a strange, blank expression on her face. She almost seemed to be sleepwalking, and she didn't speak a word. Later, Denita told us that after asking Mary if she was okay, she asked her if she wanted to go into the house. Mary merely shook her head and pointed toward Anderson and me with that blank stare. Denita then asked, "Do you want to go back there with them?" Again, Mary replied by pointing toward us, and this time she nodded her head yes, but she still did not speak.

After having a little trouble, including burning his thumb, Anderson got the fire started. We added material to the fire to make it as hot as possible, and while we busied ourselves with this, Denita watched Mary. I managed to glance at her a couple of times while I tended the fire, and she just didn't look right. She was staring into the fire as if in shock. I wasn't sure Mary should be there, but I thought that maybe she would benefit from participating in the burning of her occultic materials.

After a few minutes, Denita became cold and went inside the house. I continued to work with the fire while Anderson watched Mary. She still stood there staring blankly into the fire. Suddenly,

Mary started walking slowly toward the fire. At first Anderson and I just watched her. I guess we didn't really know what she was doing, but then we realized she was not going to stop. She was already so close to the fire that it should have been uncomfortably hot, but she kept walking toward it, just staring blankly into it, as if something in the fire was calling to her. Anderson and I realized simultaneously that Mary was not going to stop. Anderson asked her, "Why are you walking toward the fire?" In the same instant, I stepped between Mary and the fire and Anderson grabbed her arm and pulled her back.

I had planned to burn the books and then go into the house to attempt a final deliverance, but I realized I needed to take action then and there. I stood directly in front of Mary and said, "Mary, I want you to do something." She looked at me with that same blank stare. "I want you to renounce your involvement in the occult."

For the first time in quite a while, Mary spoke. "What do I say?" she asked, still staring into the fire.

"Just repeat after me," I replied, and then had her renounce her participation in occultic activities. I spoke in short phrases, and she repeated each phrase. Next I commanded the demons to leave Mary. As soon as I started talking, she bent over as if in pain. She rested her elbows on her knees and trembled. At first I thought she was sobbing, but I realized later she was not crying but shaking uncontrollably.

After commanding the demons to leave in the name of Jesus, I asked, "Are there still demons there?" My question was directed at both Mary and the demons because I had read that sometimes demons speak through the mouth of their victim. Mary nodded her head. Knowing that she had a history of self-mutilation, I asked, "Is there a demon that makes you cut yourself?" She nodded her head yes, while still bent over, trembling and breathing heavily. I then said, "I command you, demon of self-mutilation, to leave her and never return! I cast you out in the name of Jesus!" Instantly, the trembling and the heavy breathing stopped.

Mary straightened up and the blank stare was gone. In its place was a look of bewilderment. She looked all around her as if searching for somebody. Anderson asked her, "Are you okay?"

Very quietly she replied, "I'm alone."

"For the first time, right?"

"Yeah."

We learned later that Mary had no memory of the events from the time she arrived at our house that night until she realized she had no more demons. It is my firm belief that Mary was possessed during this brief period of time, and judging from the changes in her behavior and countenance following her deliverance, it was clear she had been oppressed by demonic spirits for quite some time. The next day one of the members of our congregation noticed the difference in her personality. She became more outgoing and had a certain spark that wasn't there before. We also learned later from Anderson what he meant when he told us "things got a little weird" in Mary's room. He said that when they started putting Mary's books and other articles into the box, drawers began to stick and not open and objects in the room moved around and fell over. This is when Anderson commanded the demons in Jesus' name to leave them alone.

The story with Mary did not end that night. About two weeks later I asked her how things were going and if she was still seeing spirits. Her response was a little surprising, but by now I had become accustomed to surprises and strange happenings. She said, "Not too well. One of the books we burned is under my bed."

A few days after the book burning and prayer of deliverance, Mary had begun to see spirits again, including a little girl in her kitchen. At about the same time, she discovered this book of spells under her bed. It was just barely under the bed, she emphasized. I assumed that while Anderson and Mary were placing the books into a box, Mary, under the influence of a demon, had pulled one of the books out of the box and placed it under the bed. However, I was reminded that after we burned those books, Anderson and Mary had returned to her house to thoroughly search her room and make sure all the occultic materials were gone. This search included looking under the bed. It is very unlikely they simply overlooked the book under the bed because Mary said when she found it, it was in plain sight.

I did not have an explanation for how the book got there, but I did know that Mary's deliverance could not be complete until all of her occultic materials had been destroyed, so I had Anderson bring the book home and we burned it. The next day we prayed over Mary again and commanded the demons to leave her, specifically those demons that gave her the ability to see spirits. After a few days, Anderson asked Mary if she was seeing spirits, and she said no. At long last, I believed the nightmare was finally over.

Sadly, Mary's deliverance and salvation did not completely protect her from the emotional baggage she carried. She came from an extremely dysfunctional family. She suffered from codependency, among other things, and Anderson began to see that a continued relationship with Mary could only lead to heartache for himself. He realized that if Mary eventually became his wife, the problems in her family would soon become his problems too. I was glad to see Anderson finally end the relationship, but I was a little saddened because I knew it would now be difficult for us to have any more influence over Mary. It turned out I was right, and there just was not a good way for Denita and me to maintain contact with her without her coming into contact with Anderson. It has been a while since we saw Mary, but I still pray for her. I pray that God will heal her familial relationships and take care of her.

Anderson's troubles seemed to be over once he broke up with Mary, except for one loose end that needed to be taken care of. This loose end was a consequence of the demonic influences that had now been removed. While he was living with my parents, Anderson went to a tattoo parlor to have a pentagram tattooed on his upper arm. This was to be his way of permanently protecting himself from evil spirits. I have mentioned this pentagram image before. For those unfamiliar with occultic symbology, the pentagram is a five-pointed star inside a circle that is supposed to protect the bearer. This is why Anderson was fond of necklaces bearing the pentagram. The pentagram should not be confused with the pentagraph, the image used by satanic cults. The pentagraph looks just like the pentagram except that the pentagraph's star is upside down.

As further evidence that even the emblems or objects of occultism have power over the practitioner, consider the following. Normally, a tattoo causes pain for a few days after it is first applied, but Anderson's tattoo never stopped hurting. After revealing his tattoo to us and telling us about the pain, he reminded us of something he had told us earlier, but which I had forgotten. He said that Mary once used a knife to carve a pentagram into her ankle, and thereafter she suffered pain in that area.

Anderson knew he needed to rid himself of that tattoo, and he considered having it altered by adding a new design on top of the old one. At first I thought this was a good idea, but then I started thinking how the pentagram would still be there even if he did that. I wanted the tattoo removed, if possible. Tattoo removal is accomplished through the use of lasers. It is expensive, painful, not always completely successful, can cause scarring, and usually has to be done in several treatments. Therefore, Anderson thought this was a bad idea. However, after much discussion, I convinced him to go that route for me.

When Bootsie found out about the tattoo, she informed us that she had a good friend who happened to be one of the few dermatologists in Huntsville who practiced tattoo removal. She mentioned our situation to him, and he arranged for Anderson to get an appointment within a few days. This is remarkable, because in Huntsville it typically takes months to get in to see a dermatologist for the first time. But then, due to a mix-up, Anderson did not get to have his consultation with the doctor during that initial visit. We were afraid it would be a long time before we could get him rescheduled, but when I called to talk to the doctor's receptionist and nurse, an appointment for the next day suddenly became available due to a cancellation.

Denita and I felt certain that God had come to our rescue again. Anderson was able to have the consultation with the doctor and begin his treatments, but here is the most remarkable thing that happened. Following the consultation with the doctor, the pain in the tattoo went away. It was as if Satan relented once he saw that we were intent on this course of action, and it served as a sign to me that I had made the right decision on how to remove Anderson's tattoo.

CHAPTER 12

God Speaks to Us

For most of my life I believed that when people thought God was speaking to them through dreams, visions, or voices in their head, they were just letting their imaginations run wild. I no longer believe that. I firmly believe the Holy Spirit still communicates with us in those ways. I am going to relate to you several instances of such things happening to my family. In times past, I would have attributed each of these instances to coincidence, or I would have concluded that somebody had a vivid imagination.

I have already described to you how Denita heard a voice three different times imploring her to search for something underneath Anderson's mattress and how she discovered the folder that caused us to realize we were dealing with something demonic in Anderson's life. I have also related to you how Denita had heard such a voice at various times in the past. Previously, whenever Denita would say something like "Something just told me" or "I had a very strong feeling," I wondered if that was God talking to her, because more often than not there seemed to be a very good reason for it. For example, Denita will sometimes go for months or years without thinking about somebody, and then suddenly that person is in her thoughts in a very strong way. Oftentimes she will contact this person she has been thinking about, and she will discover that the person has undergone tragedy or trauma of some sort.

I don't wonder about such occurrences anymore. I now firmly believe that this is the Spirit's way of telling Denita somebody needs her prayers and assistance. I recently asked Denita if she could describe the voice that spoke to her about looking under Anderson's mattress. I wondered whether the voice was simply a thought or something that seemed like an audible voice. She said it was definitely a voice, not just a thought. She also said she could not describe the voice. She said it sounded neither male nor female, and there was nothing outstanding about the voice, other than the fact it did not come from a human source.

In the course of my studying to understand what my family was going through, I learned that God very often communicates messages to Christians today just as He did in biblical times. This does not mean I believe God gives new doctrinal revelations outside of what is written in His Word. Instead, I believe God sometimes leads and encourages us through messages additional to the words of the Bible. I now believe without a doubt that God calls upon certain individuals to act on behalf of others who are in need, particularly when the one in need requires prayer. Please permit me to describe some events that have affected me deeply and opened my eyes to the different ways the Holy Spirit communicates with us.

The tiny congregation in which I preached for several years was about as conservative as they come, and they were not in the least ready for the things that happened to my family. The way God worked on my family and me was a source of extreme discomfort for our friends in the church. I felt like I had a new calling from God and that He had some big plans for my family, but the rest of our church did not want their boat rocked. Meanwhile, God had rocked my boat so hard I fell out of it, and now I needed Him to rescue me. I needed to be able to walk on water, so to speak, but I felt like this tiny conservative congregation was not the place to find that kind of experience with God.

After much prayer with my family, I decided we needed to go out in search of a place where Christians were not afraid to praise God openly and to give way to the presence of His Holy Spirit in their lives. I didn't know exactly what this meant, and as of this writing I still don't know exactly where God is leading me, but I knew God wasn't going to take control of my life in the presence of those who refused to believe everything He had done for my family. So we set out in search of that merciful Father of the Bible, and that compassionate Jesus, and that Comforter who is the Holy Spirit. Denita, Victoria, and I started to visit charismatic churches, something we had never done before, just to see for ourselves what they practiced. Meanwhile, Anderson began attending church with his new girlfriend. We all were in search of the Christianity we read about in Scripture.

I had my own ideas about what the New Testament church must have looked like, but recent events created doubt within me about whether I had an accurate understanding. God had showed me the fallacy of many things I once believed, so I had this feeling He was telling me I needed to reexamine every religious thing I ever believed. Therefore, whenever I visited a church that practiced some things I once believed violated Scripture, I just asked God to show me the truth. I continually asked God to show me where He wanted my family and me to be. Did He want us to join a church, or did He want us to start one?

For several months I had felt like God was putting us in a position to start a church that resembled the churches of the first century, but I was still uncertain and filled with anxiety about what He really wanted us to do. It was very uncomfortable for both Denita and me to be without a church, and we didn't know if we were doing the right thing. As we sought out the Holy Spirit, we prayed for the Lord to speak to us and show us where to go. Once again, God responded in mighty ways.

God's communication with us began, or maybe I should say continued, when we visited a church where we knew several friends and acquaintances were members. This happened just before our own small congregation disbanded. We visited this church on a Saturday night, and almost immediately upon walking through the door we ran into two of Denita's longtime friends, Jill and Rhonda. We talked with them for a few minutes in the church foyer and then went in to find a seat for the service. Denita found out later from Rhonda that as we walked away from her she heard a voice say, "The deception is being taken away." Rhonda explained to Denita that for years she had been praying for us, and often when she began to pray she heard a voice tell her to pray that our deception would be taken away. She said she never understood why she was supposed to pray that, but she obediently did so. Now we understand the deception she was praying against was the deception that prevented us from seeing how the Holy Spirit works in the lives of Christians today.

The next message we received from the Spirit came through Madela, a lady whom we had never met. We knew of Madela through our friend Bootsie. They belong to the same church. In passing one day, Bootsie told Denita about a "blessing" the church was having for Madela. God placed it upon Denita's heart to contribute a little something. A few days later Madela called Denita and left a message thanking her and expressing a desire to get together sometime. About two months later, Madela called Denita again and this time actually talked to her. Neither Denita nor I had ever spoken to Madela before this time. When Denita answered the phone that day Madela said, "Denita, this is Madela. God told me I should call you and remind you that He is the Good Shepherd. He said you were not to worry about anything in your life right now – just rest in Him and have peace." After a slight pause, Madela asked, "Denita, is everything all right?"

Madela had no idea why she called. She only knew she had been told to call Denita. Denita briefly explained to her the struggle we had been through with Anderson and how we were now trying to understand where God was leading us. God's words through Madela were very comforting to us. He told us not to fret over the fact that we didn't have a church. I believe He was telling us that He had led us into a time of rest and recovery. As He did so many times throughout our ordeal with Anderson, God showed us how He uses us all to accomplish His purpose. It was very touching to see God work through Madela to comfort us. He encouraged us to help Madela in her time of need, and then He encouraged Madela to likewise help us in our time of need. I hope you will agree with me when I say that God is awesome.

As if to drive home His point, the very next day Bootsie called Denita to tell her about a word she had received. She wasn't sure whether this was one of her own thoughts or if it was from the Lord, but she wanted Denita to hear it and make that judgment for herself. Bootsie spends time with the Lord in her house every morning. She prays to Him and meditates on His Word. She also writes down thoughts she has during her quiet time. She keeps these thoughts written in a kind of diary and hopes to publish them one day as a book of inspirational thoughts.

Bootsie says sometimes when these thoughts come to her she knows they have come from the Lord. Other times she believes they are her own thoughts, but she sometimes doesn't know the difference between what is from her and what is from the Lord. I believe on this particular day the inspirational thoughts were from the Lord because what she told Denita was so similar to what Madela had told her the day before. I have no doubt that many who read this will say Madela and Bootsie obviously collaborated on this, but they did not. These are the words of comfort the Lord gave to Bootsie on that day:

> *Don't fret—sometimes He just wants us to fish in our own pond. Relax by the calm waters. Bask in His Sonshine and listen to the words "well done good and faithful servant." [The Lord speaking] Your waters have been rough these last months. The time of calm water is a resting place readying you for ministry. Do not ripple the waters with anxiety or impatience. I calmed the sea after the storm. Rejoice in the calmness of your life. Look to the sunrise on a new day. Reflect that at dawn a lake is serene. I wish for you serenity. Bask in Me and grow strong so that when I send you out your bones will not be weary. Refresh yourself this day. As the sun rises at noon your work will commence.*

Throughout this period of time I was praying daily, and I still pray daily for God to guide me to where He wants me to be. Here I was, floating around from church to church, not knowing what to do. To make matters worse, I was supposed to be the spiritual leader of my family, and I had no idea where I was supposed to lead them! One day, I decided to take my Bible into the woods with me and ask

God to show me something that would help me. It was just a few days before Christmas, and I was enjoying some time off from work. On this particular day the weather was beautiful. The temperature had warmed into the sixties, which is unseasonably warm, even for northern Alabama.

I had read stories by men who asked God to show them something in His Word to guide them or to provide an answer to a question they had. Then they simply dropped their Bible, let it fall open, and read the first passage their eyes focused on, with astounding results. I decided to try something like that myself. So I found a relatively flat rock to sit on and began to pray. I explained to the Lord once again my plight, as if He needed to be reminded, and asked Him to show me something in His Word that would help me.

At this point in time, my spirit was vexed by the thought that maybe a charismatic church was the right place for my family to worship and serve God, so we had begun visiting them to find out what they were all about. But I was not certain God wanted me in any of these churches. I thought maybe I was doing something I wanted to do rather than what God wanted. It also concerned me that I had no way of knowing whether the Spirit was really present in any of these churches. I knew enough to know that just because a church labels itself charismatic does not mean it is truly Spirit-filled. I knew that those who had been in the charismatic movement for a while could often tell the difference between what was of the Spirit and what was of the flesh, but I was nothing but a novice.

I have to admit that as I visited various churches I was looking for spectacular evidences that they were Spirit-filled. I wanted to hear people speak in tongues and I wanted to see people healed. In other words, I was probably looking for the Holy Spirit in the wrong way. I was also struggling with the fact that these churches taught and practiced things I was not willing to embrace as scriptural, and I couldn't quite reconcile in my mind how they could be Spirit-filled if they were doing unscriptural things. So I had plenty of questions for God, and I pleaded with Him to show me something that would help.

I had walked way out on a limb, and I needed His reassurance. After several minutes of prayer I asked Him to show me a passage that would help me. I opened my Bible. The first thought I had was "Matthew," so I turned to the book of Matthew without really thinking about where I was in the book. Then I looked to the left-hand page. The page began with Matthew 6:17 and went through 7:1. I glanced at the section beginning in Matthew 6:25 where Jesus tells His followers not to worry about anything. That was a good thing for me to think about, but it didn't seem like the answer to my prayer. Then I looked at the section beginning with verse 7 in chapter 7.

I had recently studied this passage and related passages numerous times. It's the passage where Jesus says if you ask for good things the Father will not refuse your request. In Luke's account, recorded in Luke 11:9-13, it is clear that Jesus is speaking specifically of the Holy Spirit. Once again, I knew this was helpful, but I still didn't feel that this was the help I was looking for. I closed my eyes and asked God again to teach me some more. Then I opened my eyes, looked at the right-hand page, and there it was! My eyes landed right on Matthew 7:21-23: "Not everyone who says to Me, 'Lord, Lord,' shall enter the kingdom of heaven, but he who does the will of My Father in heaven. Many will say to Me in that day, 'Lord, Lord, have we not prophesied in Your name, cast out demons in Your name, and done many wonders in Your name?' And then I will declare to them, 'I never knew you; depart from Me, you who practice lawlessness!'"

When I read this passage at first it wasn't clear to me what the Spirit's message was for me, but this did seem to address the things I was most concerned about at the time and what I had been praying to God about. I thanked God for showing me this passage, then I told Him I wasn't quite sure what it meant, and I asked Him to help me understand it. I thought about that passage for a good two or three days and finally concluded what it was the Lord wanted me to understand.

Up to that point in time, I had equated the manifestation of the Spirit in a church with God's "stamp of approval" on the church, and I still believe this is generally true. But I think God wanted me to understand I should not get caught up in seeking a church with a lot of speaking in tongues, or laying on of hands, or prophesying. He was telling me not to get caught up in hype, and that the gifts of the Spirit are just one of the means to an end and not the end itself. I think God wanted me to understand that sometimes churches get so caught up in their desire to be Spirit-filled they tend to accept imitations of the Spiritual gifts.

God also reminded me of 1 Corinthians 12-14, in which Paul admonished the church in Corinth, which had genuine gifts of the Spirit, to use the gifts properly. I was reminded that the Corinthian church collectively had all of the gifts of the Spirit, but they still lacked that one thing that is more important than anything else. They lacked love. This is a concept I haven't completely grasped, but to have a spiritual gift is not necessarily to be acceptable to God. My conclusion, then, is that I should seek the Holy Spirit and allow Him to work through me in whatever fashion He chooses. I should seek to be with those who do the same, and I should seek to be with a group of believers who have the proper love for God, the truth, one another, and the lost.

Accepting the dominion of the Holy Spirit has added a dimension to my Christianity I have never known before, but I believe I have been cautioned that it is still all about Jesus Christ. The Father and the Spirit both have their glorious places in the big scheme for our redemption, but nothing at all matters without the redemptive blood of Jesus Christ. Many will claim to perform works in His name, and many will even do great things in His name, but unless they submit to His will, they will be lost.

Perhaps the most dramatic instance of God speaking to my family, since those days when He showed us how to cast out Anderson's demons, occurred fairly recently. In an earlier chapter I discussed some of the illegal activities in which Anderson was involved. I knew those evil activities could come back to haunt him one day, and it finally happened in February 2005.

Anderson was at his job at a fast food restaurant one day when the group of street racers he had once been associated with came in and asked him to restart the racing team. The team had dissolved after Anderson stopped racing. Anderson refused and they went on their way. A week later, a policeman questioned Anderson about his former involvement with the street racing team, and Anderson provided information on the other members of the team. At first it seemed like too much of a coincidence that the team members and the policeman talked to Anderson a week apart. But I now understand that Anderson and the others had been under police scrutiny for a while as they attempted to compile enough evidence to arrest them. The information Anderson provided was enough for the police to begin arresting members of the team.

Anderson was unaware that some of his old cronies had been arrested as he made plans for a Valentine's Day outing with his girl-friend and another couple. That evening, the four of them met in their church parking lot and went to dinner and then to a movie. When they came out of the theater, Anderson noticed his car was unlocked, but he assumed he just forgot to lock it before going into the theater. As Anderson drove down the street, the car started making strange noises. He had his friend take his girlfriend back to her truck in the church parking lot.

Anderson headed for home, but he didn't make it. I had already gone to sleep when Anderson called to tell me he had car trouble. He wouldn't tell me what was wrong until I got there to give him a ride home. Somebody had cut the wheel studs on one of his front wheels, and they had broken while he was driving down the street. By the grace of God, he was able to get the car off the road without wrecking. Later, we would find out about some of his former team members being arrested. It seems those who were still on the loose deduced Anderson had tipped off the police, and they sabotaged his car. Not only that, but they had broken into his car while it was parked at the movie theater and stolen items out of his glove compartment, including his vehicle registration. It was then he understood why his car was unlocked when he came out of the theater.

Just when it looked like Satan had the upper hand again, God made His presence known to us and reassured us in a very remarkable way. After a wrecker picked up Anderson's car and he and I were headed for home in my car, he told me, "You know, the really weird thing about this is I had a dream last night that tonight wouldn't work out right." He couldn't remember specifics about the dream, but it left an impression on him. Then he told me his friend had had a similar dream on the same night about their double date. In his friend's dream, a car wreck occurred during the outing, and it bothered him so much he pulled Anderson off to the side to tell him about it. Anderson then told him about his dream. Now, if you are thinking that c-word again, *coincidence*, consider the rest of the story.

I had already gone to bed that night when Anderson called to tell me he needed help. Denita was studying her Bible and praying. After Anderson came home that night and told his mom about the dreams, she related to him what happened earlier to her. She was on her way to bed when she was stricken with an overwhelming and urgent feeling that she needed to pray for Anderson. At the same time, she saw a vision of Anderson crying with his hands hand-cuffed together. She heard him say that he was so tired of it all. She had no idea what this meant at the time, but she sat down and prayed fervently for Anderson. It was just after this that Anderson called saying he needed help. I believe the Spirit had Anderson's mom pray for him just at the instant he needed help. That prayer prevented him from having a wreck and giving way to anger.

But what about the vision of Anderson in handcuffs? I think there are a couple of possibilities for how to interpret this. The first explanation is that Anderson could have become angry enough about what happened to him that he would seek revenge, which likely could have ended in his arrest or even his death. He did become very angry, and his mom and I had to talk to him for quite a while to get him to just let it go. We prayed also that God would help him control his anger. The other explanation I can think of for the vision Denita saw is that it was God's way of showing us that Anderson was still under the bondage of his previous sins because he was still suffering the consequences of his actions. Maybe God was telling Denita to pray for Anderson to endure those consequences.

After everything we have experienced, I can never again scoff at the idea that God speaks directly to people today. Sure, there are some who claim to be receiving messages from God when they really aren't, but does that make the rest of us liars? God speaks to His children, and like our own physical children, we just need to learn how to listen to our Father.

A couple of days after Anderson's car was sabotaged, the police called him and said they needed to talk to him. After he arrived at the police station, they told him they were not able to catch the entire street racing team on their first attempt. Since then, however, they had arrested the rest of the team. Anderson told them about what happened to his car a few nights before. They questioned Anderson extensively about his past and present involvement with the team. They told him they had been following him for some time and had decided he was no longer involved. That was why they had come to him for information. The police gave him a lecture on how he should never have participated in such a thing and then let him go. Once again, God showed His mercy toward Anderson.

CHAPTER 13

A New Way of Thinking

God extends His mercy to us in many ways. He forgives us of our wrongs, no matter how bad they are, and He bestows upon us many blessings we have done nothing to deserve. Through His Son, He promises us a perfect life in a perfect place, even though we can never hope to achieve perfection on our own. But there is one way God shows His mercy to us that is not obvious to many people, even Christians. God knows that we will need faith in order to be sanctified, and He is willing to give us faith and strengthen faith that is weak. Sometimes this part of God's grace can be painful.

As we see in 1 Peter 4:12, God is more than willing to allow us to suffer if He thinks it will strengthen us: "Beloved, do not think it strange concerning the fiery trial which is to try you, as though some strange thing happened to you." I am also reminded of the first chapter of Peter's first letter, where he compares strong faith to fine gold that has been purified in the fire. Yet, how many Christians in the world have never suffered even a single fiery trial? I am afraid that in America most Christians would consider it a very strange thing to be persecuted or otherwise tried.

We are so blessed in this great nation that we have become soft spiritually. You see, one problem with having everything you need or want is that it diminishes your desire for God. The effect of this is not that we stop believing in God but that we stop depending on Him. The accompanying side effect is accepting God as who we want Him to be rather than as who He says He is. I suspect that if a survey of Christians in America was conducted, we would find that a large majority would consider persecutions and other fiery trials to be bad things. But actually, if you believe Peter, we should be praying for fiery trials.

Well, I didn't ask for fiery trials, but I received them nevertheless. As the events of the past year unfolded, I felt I was being challenged by God. I believe He was, first of all, challenging me to have the courage to stand against Satan. I also believe the Lord was challenging me to reexamine my position on the nature of Satan and how he really works against us. The Lord challenged me to let Him deliver my family from Satan, to let Him take total control of my life, and to allow Him to lead. He also challenged me to humble myself before Him. By allowing me to undergo trials, He put me in a position to make Psalm 116, the psalm referred to by the apostle Paul in 2 Corinthians 4:13, a personal song of praise to Him. I give thanks to the Spirit for helping Denita take note of this passage so she would bring it to my attention. As you read this passage, please understand that this is the way God lifts us to new heights in His kingdom. He allows us to suffer pain as a way of getting our attention and increasing our dependence on Him. He waits for us to call upon Him to deliver us and lift us up; He does lift us up in a mighty way and makes us stronger than we were before. Listen as the psalmist sings:

> I love the Lord, because He has heard
> My voice and my supplications.
> Because He has inclined His ear to me,
> Therefore I will call upon Him as long as I live.
>
> The pains of death surrounded me,
> And the pangs of Sheol laid hold of me;
> I found trouble and sorrow.
> Then I called upon the name of the Lord:
> "O Lord, I implore You, deliver my soul!"

Gracious is the Lord, and righteous;
Yes, our God is merciful.
The Lord preserves the simple;
I was brought low, and He saved me.
Return to your rest, O my soul,
For the Lord has dealt bountifully with you.

For You have delivered my soul from death,
My eyes from tears,
And my feet from falling.
I will walk before the Lord
In the land of the living.
I believed, therefore I spoke,
"I am greatly afflicted."
I said in my haste,
"All men are liars."

What shall I render to the Lord
For all His benefits toward me?
I will take up the cup of salvation,
And call upon the name of the Lord.
I will pay my vows to the Lord
Now in the presence of all His people.

Precious in the sight of the Lord
Is the death of His saints.

O Lord, truly I am Your servant;
I am Your servant, the son of Your maidservant;
You have loosed my bonds.
I will offer to You the sacrifice of thanksgiving,
And will call upon the name of the Lord.

I will pay my vows to the Lord
Now in the presence of all His people,
In the courts of the Lord's house,
In the midst of you, O Jerusalem.

Praise the Lord!

Reading this passage reminds me that when God allows us to be tested, it is for the purpose of being drawn closer to Him, and it makes us more apt to praise Him. I feel honored that God would choose to submit me to such a trial as I've been through so He can enjoy my praise. I love Him for challenging me. I love Him most of all for His challenge to reexamine my position on the nature of the Holy Spirit and how He works in our lives. Achieving a deeper understanding of the Holy Spirit might not seem like an obvious outgrowth of my family's struggle with Satan's darkness, but as I studied scriptures about demons and about our Christ-given authority to cast them out, I was also forced to deal with what the Bible teaches about the Spirit and His gifts. I would now like to share with you the thought process I went through once I realized I had the authority to cast out demons in the name of Christ. This led me to praise the Lord like I never have before and to live out Psalm 116 in my life.

I had studied the Holy Spirit on various occasions in the past, but I always approached these studies within the context of my own paradigm, which caused me to dismiss all the scriptures concerning the supernatural working of the Holy Spirit as verses that do not apply to us today. But God, through His wonderful mercy, showed me how to break out of that restrictive paradigm. I have already briefly discussed how I had to read Jesus' Great Commission to the apostles in Mark 16:17-18 from a new perspective once I realized my son's problems were demonic. This was not an easy thing for me to do, and I can't tell you how many times I have read and reread verses 15-18 trying to work out a way for that passage to tell me, yes, Jesus gave us the authority to cast out demons in His name, but, no, He did not give us the authority to lay hands on the sick or to speak in tongues.

Go into all the world and preach the gospel to every crea-ture. He who believes and is baptized will be saved; but he who does not believe will be condemned. And these signs will follow those who believe: In my name they will cast out demons; they will speak with new tongues; they will take up serpents; and if they drink anything deadly, it will by no means hurt them; they will lay hands on the sick, and they will recover.

I came to accept all of the truths about Jesus' promises in these verses, but it didn't happen all at once. Because of the order of events, I fairly readily accepted that Jesus really did promise us the authority to cast out demons. Then, a few months later when the Lord healed Denita, I saw for the first time in my life a dramatic healing, so I knew the promise of healing through the laying on of hands must be true. After that we actually laid our hands on Victoria, prayed for her, and she received healing. For many people I know, it is much easier to believe God will answer a prayer and heal somebody than to believe that healing can occur as the result of hands being laid upon the sick. But I can see very little difference between the two. A miracle is a miracle. My belief that Jesus promised miraculous healing for His believers was reinforced by the many modern stories of healing I read as the story I've related to you unfolded. As I began to read stories of deliverance from demons I quickly noticed that those who were knowledgeable of such things were also very familiar with miraculous healing. I also learned that, just as in New Testament times, many modern physical maladies are actually caused by demons.

As I studied this topic of healing from a fresh perspective, I encountered evidence of God's miraculous intervention in modern times. The evidence has always been there; I just never bothered to look for it. As I've stated previously, I used to interpret Mark 16:17-18 as a reference to the believers of the first century because I could not accept that the miraculous gifts of the Holy Spirit, the working of miracles, demon possession, and casting out demons lasted beyond the age of the apostles. But in this passage Jesus puts no time limit on His promise. Compare this to verse 16, where Jesus promises that "he who believes and is baptized will be saved; but he who does not believe will be condemned." Was this a limited-time offer by the Lord? Of course not. This offer stands for all time.

Mark 16:17-18 has for many years caused problems for me. I rejected any evidence of demon possession, casting out of demons, speaking in tongues, and miraculous healing without even investigating the facts. I proclaimed for many years, "The age of miracles is over." When presented with evidence of modern miracles, I explained it away. I made the claim that the baptism of the Holy Spirit, with its accompanying miraculous gifts, could only be passed along by the laying on of the apostles' hands. Therefore, when all of the apostles and those on whom they had laid their hands were gone, the miraculous gifts ceased.

I also developed theories tying the end of demon possession to the end of the miraculous gifts. For instance, I once believed that demonic activity was one of the ways Satan attempted to stop the growth of Christianity, and for some reason those attacks ceased at a later time. I believed the miracles were allowed to happen as a way of countering Satan's attacks, but that they were no longer needed once the threat was gone.

One particular passage in the New Testament illustrates that the statement "the miraculous gifts of the Holy Spirit could only be administered by the laying on of the apostles' hands" is false. In the account of Saul's (Paul's) conversion in Acts 9, we read that Saul received the Holy Spirit when Ananias laid his hands on him. Nowhere do we read that Ananias was an apostle. So the miraculous gifts of the Holy Spirit could also be administered by the laying on of hands of ordinary Christians! This passage was a personal bombshell.

I became further convinced that modern miracles can and do happen when the Lord led me to written references by some of the early church fathers. These documents reveal the casting out of demons and the working of the Holy Spirit much later than the first century A.D. For example, in A.D. 165, Justin Martyr wrote the following:

> For numberless demoniacs throughout the whole world, and in your city, many of our Christian men exorcising them in the name of Jesus Christ, who was crucified under Pontius Pilate, have healed and do heal, rendering helpless and driving the possessing devils out of the men, though they could not be cured by all the other exorcists, and those who used

incantations and drugs.[1]

In A.D. 200 Irenaeus wrote the following:

Wherefore, also, those who are in truth His disciples, receiving grace from Him, do in His name perform [miracles], so as to promote the welfare of other men, according to the gift which each one has received from Him. For some do certainly and truly drive out devils, so that those who have thus been cleansed from evil spirits frequently both believe [in Christ], and join themselves to the Church. Others have foreknowledge of things to come: they see visions, and utter prophetic expressions. Others still, heal the sick by laying their hands upon them, and they are made whole. Yea, moreover, as I have said, the dead even have been raised up, and remained among us for many years.[2]

Also in A.D. 200, Tertullian wrote the following:

How many men of rank (to say nothing of common people) have been delivered from devils, and healed of diseases![3]

In A.D. 250, Origen wrote this:

And some give evidence of their having received through this faith a marvelous power by the cures which they perform, invoking no other name over those who need their help than that of the God of all things, and of Jesus, along with a mention of His history. For by these means we too have seen many persons freed from grievous calamities, and from distractions of mind, and madness, and countless other ills, which could be cured neither by men nor devils.[4]

The following is often attributed to Clement of Alexandria but likely was written by an unknown author around A.D. 275:

Let them, therefore, with fasting and with prayer make their adjurations. . . as men who have received the gift of healing from God, confidently, to the glory of God.[5]

Lactantius, around the year A.D. 300, wrote this:

And as He Himself before His passion put to confusion demons by His word and command, so now, by the name and sign of the same passion, unclean spirits, having insinuated themselves into the bodies of men, are driven out, when racked and tormented, and confessing themselves to be demons, they yield themselves to God, who harasses them.[6]

If these are accurate accounts of the events of the day, miracles and deliverance from demons were common long after all the apostles, and even all upon whom the apostles laid their hands, had died. There are a few other references to spiritual gifts in the third century and beyond. These references created serious doubt in my mind about the validity of my argument that spiritual gifts died out with those who had the apostles' hands laid upon them. However, I do not need to know what the church fathers wrote to believe that my son was afflicted by demons. Denita had pain and fatigue for years, she prayed for God to heal her, and within an hour she was healed. Her pain and fatigue have never returned. There were no drugs involved and no doctors. Only prayer was used.

A miracle is commonly defined as something that occurs in defiance of the laws of nature. If what happened to Denita was not a miracle, it could only have been a coincidence. The possibility that it was a coincidence is practically zero, because people don't just instantly stop having arthritis and fibromyalgia for natural reasons. For Denita and Victoria both to have gotten well purely by accident, just after prayer, would have been quite a coincidence indeed.

In the meantime, while I was becoming acquainted with deliverance and healing stories, I couldn't avoid the fact that those who cast out demons and laid hands on others also spoke in tongues. Therefore, I launched into a study of tongues and a study of Holy Spirit baptism. In the end, together with my dear wife, who read all of the same books with me, I concluded that all of Jesus' promises in Mark 16:17-18 and the baptism of the Holy Spirit are still in effect today.

I now believe that the "days of miracles" did nearly end when the church went from a loosely organized body of believers who assembled together in small numbers, primarily in houses, to a much more structured organization. The church, in this more organized form, was forced by the church leadership to assemble together in large gatherings. When the church assembled in small numbers, a great deal of emphasis was placed on ministering to one another and unbelieving neighbors through the gifts of the Holy Spirit.

As the church became a more structured organization the clergy kept a watchful eye on the activities of Christians. Under this new arrangement, I believe Christians were forced to give up their dependence on the Holy Spirit and instead looked to the clergy for all their spiritual needs. In essence, I believe the gifts of the Spirit went away not because God took them away but because Christians simply stopped desiring and using them.

I knew from the beginning there was no honest way to interpret Mark 16:15-18 properly as long as I studied with a closed mind and clung tenaciously to my belief that the "days of miracles" were over. It wasn't easy, but I did get over that hurdle, and now I firmly believe that the promises Jesus makes in verses 17-18 are in effect today just as His promise in verse 16, which says, "He who believes and is baptized will be saved."

Like most with my religious background, I was once very willing to put a partition between verses 16 and 17 because I firmly believed Christians today couldn't cast out demons or speak in tongues or effectively lay hands on the sick. I knew there were many who claimed to do these things, but I never even bothered to investigate the truth of the claims. I simply dismissed them. I hope and pray that somebody reading this will learn the lesson I learned without having to pay the painful cost I paid. I now understand that I can never again interpret Scripture so carelessly. I once prided myself on the amount of thorough research I put into my understanding of the Scriptures. I had even reached some conclusions that were contrary in a fairly dramatic way to the doctrine of those with whom I fellowshipped for years. But God, through His incomprehensible mercy, saw that I needed to be humbled. He showed me how I was really no better than many I had condemned for interpreting scriptures to fit their preconceived ideas.

So now I understand what message is really being conveyed at the end of Mark 16. Jesus promised His apostles that when they went out into the world and taught the gospel, those who believed and were baptized would be saved. And then, contrary to what I once believed, He promised that those same believers would have certain distinguishing abilities. They would be able to cast out demons, speak in new tongues, survive snakebite and poisoning, and be able to heal the sick by laying their hands on them. In the past, I was always willing to accept the permanence of the promise that those who believe and are baptized will be saved, and I now understand that the promise of the signs that will follow those who believe is just as permanent. I wonder now how I ever accepted that Jesus' first promise stands for as long as the world is here, but that the second promise of the signs accompanying the believers had a time limit on it. No such time limit is even implied in what Jesus says, and there is no break between verses 16 and 17.

Be that as it may, plenty of well-meaning theologians and preachers are supplied with some very good-sounding arguments for why the Holy Spirit does not bestow spiritual gifts today. At one time I had no problem believing these arguments. In fact, my primary argument against the miraculous working of the Holy Spirit today was that I just didn't see it happening. But now I have a whole new way of thinking. I have actually cast out demons in the name of Jesus, so I have my own personal confirmation that Jesus' promise on that subject was true and is still in effect. And now I understand that I can't separate that promise from the other promises Jesus made. If I can cast out demons, then I should also be able to speak in tongues and bring about healing through the laying on of my hands. In addition, I now accept that I should not fear death in the line of Christian duty whether it be from snakebite, poisoning, or from some other natural cause.

Once I became properly oriented on Mark 16:15-18, I was prepared to study 1 Corinthians 12-14 in a new light. It is amazing how much more focused your study of a passage can become once you accept that it is something that might have direct meaning for you. Just a few short months ago, even after I had become fully convinced of my empowerment to cast out demons in Jesus' name, I was still arguing that the only speaking in tongues that takes place today is gibberish that arises from an assembly of people being worked into a frenzied emotional state. I was totally ignorant of the fact that the apostle Paul actually spoke of two types of tongues. One type was given by the Spirit to enhance a Christian's personal prayer life, and a second was meant to be a public sign to unbelievers through accompanying interpretation.

In the past I always assumed Paul was discussing only the latter form of tongues in his letters. I thought this because I had never researched the subject. I had never interviewed anybody who spoke in tongues to understand their beliefs, and I had never bothered to read any books on the subject. But once I did those things I found out there are many stories by many reputable people providing convincing evidence of tongues being spoken in ways that are in keeping with Paul's teachings.

I once believed 1 Corinthians 13:10 teaches us that when "that which is perfect" (the New Testament) was finalized and became widely available, there was no more need for miraculous gifts and they passed away. I now realize interpreting this passage in such a way was just a case of wishful thinking. This interpretation contradicts the theory that the age of miracles ceased once those who had received the spiritual gifts by the laying on of the apostles' hands were gone. All who had received the Holy Spirit from the apostles would have been gone by late in the second century, and the New Testament was not officially canonized until the middle of the fourth century.

Thinking about this further, why did the New Testament have to be organized as such in order for the prophecy in 1 Corinthians 13:10 to be fulfilled? The writings that make up the New Testament were all circulated among the churches from the day they were written by the inspired writers. Many of the writings were compiled by the end of the first century in collections that very closely resembled the New Testament. These were later accepted as canonical. So the church had all of the perfect truths taught in the New Testament from the first century on. Did the church have to officially declare the collection of twenty-seven writings as "the New Testament" in order for it to be perfect? I concluded the answer to that question is "no, of course not."

I found further evidence to convince me I had misinterpreted 1 Corinthians 13:10. If "that which is perfect" refers to the canonized New Testament, we should not see the gifts of the Spirit occurring in the church after about the middle of the fourth century. But in fact what we see is that the record of miracles and casting out of demons continues well beyond that time. What is perhaps the best example of this in ancient times is found in Augustine of Hippo's *City of God*, Book 22, Chapter 8.[7] Augustine, who had most of his life believed that miracles ceased with the passing of the apostles, witnessed a flurry of miraculous activity in the church in his later years. He even kept records of miracles, along with affidavits from physicians, so there would be written evidence that could be used to convince non-believers.

But now I would like to skip ahead in time approximately fourteen hundred years and consider Barton W. Stone's eyewitness account of the things that happened during some of the great revival meetings in America in the early 1800s. Barton W. Stone was one of the preachers who began a fairly large movement to lead people away from denominational creeds and into a fellowship that accepted the Bible as its only guide, and which taught that Christ died for only one church and not for multiple denominations. The aim of the movement was the restoration of New Testament Christianity, thus it was called the Restoration Movement. It was a very conservative movement which led to the formation of a few churches that insisted the age of miracles and the miraculous indwelling of the Holy Spirit, among other things, ended with the passing of the apostles. Those who are not familiar with the history of the Christian Church, Disciples of Christ, and Churches of Christ probably are not familiar with either Barton W. Stone or the Restoration Movement.

In all my years of studying the Restoration Movement, reading about Barton W. Stone, and being taught about him, I had never read his autobiography. Denita and I were introduced to this autobiography by Doug Mann. We read about how Barton W. Stone witnessed what would in New Testament times be called gifts or workings of the Spirit, but which in the early nineteenth century were referred to as "exercises." These exercises consisted of people speaking in tongues, prophesying, falling to the ground (known today as being slain in the Spirit), jerking, dancing, barking, laughing uncontrollably, and other such activities. If you read this chapter in Stone's autobiography you see that while he thought many of the things he saw were simply the result of excitement on the part of the participants, he thought most of it was beneficial to the awakening movement of that time. He described the most remarkable of these "exercises" he witnessed this way:

> I shall close this chapter with the singing exercise. This is more unaccount than any thing else I ever saw. The subject in a very happy state of mind would sing most melodiously, not from the mouth or nose, but entirely from the breast, the sounds issuing thence. Such music silenced every thing, and attracted the attention of all. It was most heavenly. None could ever be tired of hearing it. Doctor J. P. Campbell and myself were together at a meeting and were attending to a pious lady thus exercised, and concluded it to be something surpassing any thing we had known in nature.[8]

There are many more written accounts of gifts of the Spirit being manifest, and miracles being performed, and demons being cast out throughout the sixteen hundred years since the New Testament canon was established, but I will not go into those. The things that have happened to my family are reason enough for me to believe that I must reject my long-held interpretation of 1 Corinthians 13:8-10. Instead, I favor an interpretation that says "that which is perfect" is the state of bliss we achieve in heaven when love in its purest form will be experienced by all of the saved. At that time there will be no need for miraculous gifts, whose purpose was to prepare us for heaven.

Even though I have come to a more complete understanding of

how Satan battles against God's children, and of the promises made by Jesus to His children, and how those promises are fulfilled through the Holy Spirit within us, there is one area where I still seek understanding. I will preface what I am about to say by declaring that it might be the legalistic part of me that is causing my confusion. I was raised among a group of believers who have a great regard and respect for the Bible as God's infallible Word, and who emphasize that each individual is responsible for achieving a proper understanding of what is in God's Word, because we will each be judged individually on that last great day when the sheep and the goats are separated.

To that end, we have studied for many years to achieve the best possible understanding of the Word that we can. I still believe this to be the best approach to learning what God's will is for mankind and for us as individuals. However, many people have turned this search for truth in the Word into a legalistic formulation of "thou shalts" and "thou shalt nots" as in the Old Law of Moses, and it may be that I was one of those.

I believe I could sit down with my Bible and a concordance right now and go through a fairly exhaustive study of relevant Bible topics with anyone who cared to study with me. But when it comes to living a life of pure faith, love, and generosity toward my fellow man, and openly praising the Lord daily in word and deed, I know I have always been lacking, and the same is true of many in the Christian world. If we could find the proper balance between a knowledge of "book, chapter, and verse" and the fervent zeal God expects from us, what a dynamic force we would be in the world!

Because of the things that have happened to my family, I believe God is working a transition in me. He is taking me from the state of almost emotionless and legalistic pursuit of truth into a state of overflowing joy in the Lord based on a scriptural understanding of what He has done for me and what He expects from me. But as God works this transition in me, I am struggling with something. Many of those through whom the Holy Spirit seems to be working don't appear to be in complete agreement with the Scriptures on certain topics such as what it takes to be saved and the organization, government, and functioning of the church.

For example, because of the evidence I have either read, heard, or seen, I cannot refute that the Holy Spirit is active among those who have various beliefs on what form baptism should take and what role it plays in salvation. I have concluded from the things I recently learned that the Holy Spirit is manifesting His presence and power through some of those who believe baptism is pouring a little water on a baby's head, but that He also gives gifts to those who believe baptism means complete immersion in water. The Spirit also bestows gifts upon those who believe baptism is essential for salvation as well as those who believe it is merely an outward sign of belief and of salvation that has already taken place.

The Bible can't possibly teach that all of these forms of baptism are correct, and I doubt very seriously that the Lord left it up to us to decide for ourselves what baptism is. He goes to great lengths in the New Testament to describe the function of baptism, the form it takes, and the role it plays in the salvation experience, leaving me with the belief that Ephesians 4:5 means exactly what it says when it declares there is "one Lord, one faith, one baptism." Yet, I know of many accounts of the Holy Spirit working miraculously in the lives of people with every conceivable notion of what baptism is.

So I ask this question about Ephesians 4:5 and other passages. If the Holy Spirit guided men to describe to us in detail something as fundamental as baptism, why does He then accept any and all forms men choose to practice? I want you to understand that when I ask such questions, I am not questioning whether the Holy Spirit is actually working through Christians in many different churches. I believe He is because the evidence is overwhelming, and I am not going to take the stand, as many have, that this cannot be so because all of those people aren't in strict compliance with scriptural teachings on the role of baptism in salvation. I am, however, praying to God that He will cause me to understand the true role of Scripture versus the true role of the Holy Spirit in our lives. I am praying that I will be able to reconcile what I see happening—the Holy Spirit working miracles through members of many churches having very different beliefs—with my belief that the Bible is holy and infallible and God's authoritative guidance for His body of believers.

So far, the only explanation I have found is that the Lord is looking for those who will give themselves over to Him wholly, those who will depend on Him for everything rather than looking to the world or to themselves. The fact that a person hasn't come to a full understanding of what baptism is may not be grounds for God dismissing him from His saving grace. After all, we know that none of us will get into heaven based on perfect obedience. If that is the criterion for going to heaven, we might as well give up today. As much as I believe in the importance of understanding and obeying God's will and in doing good works, I also know that it is only through His grace and the saving blood of Jesus that I will live eternally with Him.

I would not ask anybody to believe there is overwhelming evidence of the Holy Spirit working through Christians today, or of demon possession, or of modern miracles, by simply taking my word for it. I encourage you to examine the evidence and decide for yourself what is the truth. Pay close attention when your friends and acquaintances talk about the miracles they've seen, and take the time to ask them questions about their experiences. I also encourage you to read as much as you can. Yes, it is true that you can't believe everything you read, but please don't use that as your excuse for not believing. Consider that most Christians who write about their experiences do not do so for selfish reasons. You must be open-minded because if you are not, you will likely not arrive at the truth and you will still be stuck in your prejudices, whether they are justified or not.

As an aid in your own personal research, I have provided a suggested reading list in an appendix. These are the books Denita and I read as we were trying to reach an understanding of the things God was showing us during our recent experiences. I do not claim that these are the best books to read on demons, modern miracles, and the working of the Holy Spirit today, and this is most certainly not an exhaustive list of all books available on the subject. These are just the books that God led us to read.

CHAPTER 14

Please Believe

I know that by telling this story I will alienate some friends. In fact, I already have. I share a common religious background with many who are not going to readily accept the truth about demonic activities and occultic bondage, although I pray they will accept it. They will read the things in this book and will not be willing to research the many other accounts of demonic oppression, obsession, and possession that have been recorded over the years. They also will not be willing to research the many, many documented accounts of the miraculous workings of the Holy Spirit in modern times. Instead, they will attempt to use their Bibles to prove that these things can't happen today.

This has already happened in our little church, where I made no secret of the fact that we had battled demons and that God had worked miracles of healing in my family. Through my naiveté, I guess I really expected our friends in the church to rejoice with us and join us in praise to God for all the things He did for us. Instead, there was nothing, not even a "Wow!" I tried not to feel disappointed, but I felt that way nevertheless. Once our ordeal was finally over, I tried to go on as if everything was normal, but everything was far from normal.

As time went on, I gradually introduced into my sermons and Bible studies some of the new beliefs I was developing on the Holy

Spirit. Finally, with some prompting from Denita, I decided the time had come to just lay everything on the table. I prepared a study on the Holy Spirit and began going through it with the church. However, I was challenged with an argument that the Bible provides evidence that the days of miracles ended at the destruction of Jerusalem in A.D. 70. I had never heard this particular argument before, and in an earlier time I might have found it somewhat convincing. But no argument against spiritual power, good or evil, in modern times is going to be very convincing to me now because every such argument ignores the reality.

Those who make these arguments are well meaning, but it is very sad to me that people will go to such great lengths to rationalize away something when they know nothing about it. I used to be the same way, so I pray for those who make such arguments. I pray that God will open their eyes just as He has opened mine. These friends of mine who will rationalize away the truth about what has happened to my family will likely label me as a fanatic, among other things, and many will no doubt refuse to fellowship with me over this issue. I am sorry it will happen that way, but I know it will because I know the attitudes of those to whom I refer. But I can never stop telling this story.

Consider this. If you discovered one day that you had the cure for some terrible disease, wouldn't you want to get the news to everybody you know, and wouldn't you want to give that cure to every victim of the disease you could find? If God healed you of some dreadful disease, wouldn't you want to praise His name and tell the story to everyone you know? Well, God has done wonderful things for my family. He has performed both physical and spiritual healing, and I cannot cease praising Him.

Also, I have learned that all Christians have the cure for a most dreadful spiritual disease. I now know what that cure is and how to use it. By God's will, and through His grace, I intend to apply this cure at every opportunity I have. I intend to teach this message in the hope that others will take heed, and I hope to seek out those who have been involved in witchcraft and other occultic activities and have come under occultic bondage. Also, I will continue to pray that teenagers and their parents everywhere will take seriously the dangers of even casual contact with the occult. It is my intent, at every opportunity, to encourage teenagers and young adults to not be lured into witchcraft by its promises of excitement and adventure. I pray that every single person who reads this will understand that witchcraft and other occultic activities are not innocent fun, but that through such activities Satan can take a person's soul captive. Satan is destroying many souls through the occult, and by refusing to believe that Satan is using his demons in such a way we allow him an easy victory.

I also now understand that a personal relationship with the Holy Spirit, which I had always discounted before, is possible. I know now He works great wonders through God's people and gives us many gifts. I now believe that a Christian cannot completely experience the joy of being in Christ without accepting God in His completeness. The full Christian experience comes through accepting the Father, the Son, and the Spirit totally on God's terms. I pray that those who do not believe a personal relationship with the Spirit is possible will take the time to honestly research the topic and reach a conclusion based on objective, open-minded searching rather than on preconceived notions.

I pray that you will not rationalize away the things you have read in this book. Just a little over a year ago, if I had heard a story like the one in which my family has been involved, I likely would have rationalized that all of these events have a natural explanation. My tendency to do that went away the day my son told me he could see spirits. As a means of illustrating why I feel it is so important to tell this story, allow me to tell you something we have recently learned about somebody we know. I will leave out most of the details in order to protect the person's privacy, but we know a person who hears voices. This person is sometimes threatened and terrorized by these voices. This person has come to believe these voices have no real authority over her, but she does not believe the voices are created in her mind by demons who can be cast out.

I cannot overemphasize to you that there are many, many recorded cases of people hearing such voices until their demons were cast out. Most people who suffer from this are diagnosed as being schizophrenic, and possibly rightly so. But some suffer from demonic oppression, and no one ever attempts to exorcise demons from them. How many people are suffering needless mental anguish because they refuse to believe they could be under demonic attack? If you take nothing else from the things I've written, I hope you will believe God has given us the authority to perform great works in the name of Jesus. There are certain things He will not do for us. There are certain instances in which He expects us to take action. Please don't refuse to accept the authority God has given you.

I rejoice every day in the Lord and give Him all the glory and praise, for all the things He has taught me and for the magnificent display of His tremendous power my family has seen. I praise Him for having mercy on someone as unworthy as I am. I praise Him for showing me the many books containing such convincing evidence that thousands of cases of demonic influence and occultic bondage have been overcome in recent history by the blood of Jesus and through those who are not afraid to cast out demons in Jesus' name. I praise Him for showing me so much evidence of the miraculous intervention of the Spirit in the lives of modern Christians.

My faith has soared as a result of the events of the past few months. I finally see after all these years that there really is a war being waged between the spiritual forces of good and evil, and that the battleground is our minds and souls. I praise God for His Son, who loved us all enough to die on the cross for us and to win the victory over Satan through His resurrection. I praise God for raising Jesus, for the saving power of Jesus' blood, and for the power it has over every kind of evil. I thank God for teaching me that by the power of the blood of Jesus I can do battle against Satan and win.

Endnotes

Chapter 3 The Day My World Was Redefined
1. Joe Beam, *Seeing the Unseen: A Handbook on Spiritual Warfare* (West Monroe, La.: Howard Publishing, 1996).

Chapter 4 Spirits in My Parents' House?
1. Kurt E. Koch, *Occult Bondage and Deliverance: Counseling the Occultly Oppressed* (Grand Rapids, Mich.: Kregel Publications, 1970).

Chapter 5 My Son Leaves Home
1. Lester Sumrall, *Witch Doctor* (South Bend, Ind.: LeSEA Publishing, 1988).

2. Kurt E. Koch, *Demonology Past and Present: Identifying and Overcoming Demonic Strongholds* (Grand Rapids, Mich.: Kregel Publications, 1973).

Chapter 8 A Demon in the Car
Don Basham, *Deliver Us From Evil: The Story of a Man Who Dared to Explore the Censored Fourth of Christ's Ministry* (Grand Rapids, Mich.: Chosen Books, 1972).

Chapter 13 A New Way of Thinking

1. Edited by Alexander Roberts, D.D. & James Donaldson, LL.D., revised by A. Cleveland Coxe, D.D., *The Writings of the Fathers Down to A.D. 325, Ante-Nicene Fathers*, Volume 1, (Peabody, Mass.: Hendrickson Publishers, 2004), 190.

2. Ibid., Volume 1, 409.

3. Ibid., Volume 3, 107.

4. Ibid., Volume 4, 473.

5. Ibid., Volume 8, 59.

6. Ibid., Volume 7, 243.

7. Internet Christian Library website, http://www.iclnet.org/, "City of God," Book 22, Chapter 8 found at http://ccel.org/fathers NPNF1-02/Augustine/cog/t123.htm#t123.htm.3.

8. http://www.mun.ca/rels/restmov/texts/bstone/barton.html, "A Short History of the Life of Barton W. Stone, Written by Himself (1847)," [based on the edition in *Voices from Cane Ridge*, edited by Rhodes Thompson, St. Louis Mo.: The Bethany Press, 1954, 31-134. Transcribed by Paul Woodhouse; HTML by Mike Stewart].

APPENDIX

Other Suggested Reading

Basham, Don, *Deliver Us From Evil: The Story of a Man Who Dared to Explore the Censored Fourth of Christ's Ministry*, Grand Rapids: Chosen, 1972.

Basham, Don, *Face Up With a Miracle*, Springdale: Whitaker, 1967.

Basham, Don, *A Handbook on Holy Spirit Baptism*, New Kensington: Whitaker, 1969.

Bredesen, Harald, with James F. Scheer, *Need a Miracle?*, Tulsa: Harrison, 1979.

Bredesen, Harald, with Pat King, *Yes Lord*, Tulsa: Harrison, 1982.

Hull, Bill, *Straight Talk on Spiritual Power: Experiencing the Fullness of God in the Church*, Grand Rapids: Baker, 2002.

Miller, Duane, *Out of the Silence, A Personal Testimony of God's Healing Power*, Nashville: Thomas Nelson, 1996.

Prince, Derek, *Baptism in the Holy Spirit*, New Kensington: Whitaker, 1995.

Prince, Derek, *Blessing or Curse, You Can Choose: Freedom From Pressures You Thought You Had to Live With*, Grand Rapids: Chosen, 2000.

Prince, Derek, *Spiritual Warfare*, New Kensington: Whitaker, 1987.

Sherrill, John L., *They Speak with Other Tongues*, Tarrytown: Revell, 1985 (no longer in print).

Stewart, Don, *Only Believe: An Eyewitness Account of the Great Healing Revivals of the 20th Century*, Shippensburg: Destiny Image, 1999.

Sumrall, Lester, *Demons, the Answer Book*, New Kensington: Whitaker, 2003.

Sumrall, Lester, *Alien Entities: A Look Behind the Door to the Spirit Realm*, Springdale: Whitaker, 1995.

Sumrall, Lester, *The Gifts and Ministries of the Holy Spirit*, New Kensington: Whitaker, 1982.

Sumrall, Dr. Lester, *101 Questions & Answers on Demon Powers*, South Bend: Sumrall, 1983.

Sumrall, Lester, *Bitten By Devils: The Supernatural Account of a Young Girl Bitten by Unseen Demons, Documented by Medical Doctors & Her Miraculous Deliverance That Would Bring Revival to a Nation*, South Bend: LeSEA, 1987.

Sumrall, Dr. Lester, *Study Guide, Indiana University, Human Illness & Divine Healing*, South Bend: Sumrall, 2001.

CPSIA information can be obtained
at www.ICGtesting.com
Printed in the USA
LVOW12s1941051016

507576LV00003B/67/P